BALANCE IN MOTION

Ivan Boszormenyi-Nagy and His Vision of
Individual and Family Therapy

BALANCE IN MOTION

Ivan Boszormenyi-Nagy and His Vision of Individual and Family Therapy

By

Ammy van Heusden

and

ElseMarie van den Eerenbeemt

BRUNNER/MAZEL *Publishers* • New York

Library of Congress Cataloging-in-Publication Data

Heusden, Ammy van, d. 1986.
  Balance in motion.

  Translation of: Balans in beweging.
  "Appendix B: Bibliography of works by Ivan
Boszormenyi-Nagy, M.D.": p. 115
  1. Contextual therapy. 2. Boszormenyi-Nagy, Ivan,
1920–   I. Eerenbeemt, ElseMarie van den. II. Title.
RC488.55.H4813 1987   616.89'14   87-10379
ISBN 0-87630-469-2

Dutch edition, *Balans in beweging Ivan Boszormenyi-Nagy en zijn visie op individuele en gezinstherapie,* published by UITGEVERIJ DE TOORTS, Haarlem, Holland © 1983 by Ammy van Heusden, ElseMarie van den Eerembeemt, and Ivan Boszormenyi-Nagy

English edition © 1987 by Ammy van Heusden, ElseMarie van den Eerenbeemt, and Ivan Boszormenyi-Nagy

Published by
BRUNNER/MAZEL, INC.
19 Union Square
New York, New York 10003

MANUFACTURED IN THE UNITED STATES OF AMERICA
10 9 8 7 6 5 4 3 2 1

CONTENTS

FOREWORD

The Contextual approach to therapy integrates elements of classical individual and family therapies. It aims at an integrated healing leverage coming from the advanced understanding of relational consequences beyond both psychological-individual determinants and transactional-feedback. The fullest understanding of relationships and therapeutic leverages will require a new synthesis of concepts and methods, somewhat parallel to the idea of structural violence in social science, a concept that transcends both individual and immediate transactional explanations.

It was no surprise to me that a genuine interest in such synthesizing understanding would evolve first in the Netherlands, a country with a rich progressive heritage. My 22 years of continuing exchanges with Dutch colleagues have confirmed my impression of a courage to explore new frontiers combined with a respect for the individual in an increasingly mechanized and depersonalized world.

Ammy van Heusden has a prominent place in the history of Dutch family therapy. I first met her in Philadelphia during her study trip to America in 1965. Ever since, she has provided continuous leadership through initiating programs and training a multitude of Dutch and foreign students. Hers was an invaluable contribution to the program development of the nationwide three-month training program, conducted by myself and two of my colleagues, Drs. Gerald M. Zuk and David Rubinstein, from the Department of Family Psychiatry of Eastern Pennsylvania

Psychiatric Institute, held in Leiden in 1967. This early effort and
Ammy's teaching contributions at the advanced social work level
helped to establish Holland as the European forerunner of
family therapy.

I always found Ammy to be an open-minded, profoundly concerned professional with the vision to recognize and adopt new
avenues for helping people. She showed a consistent interest in
human relationships beyond the confines of obvious transactional connections and simple symptom removal. I am pleased
and complimented by her enduring interest in my work, and I
deeply mourn her passing in April of 1986. In a way this book is
part of her legacy to posterity and its publication in English was
her last wish.

I have known ElseMarie van den Eerenbeemt for some six
years. I first met her in connection with her work with under-
privileged families in the tough neighborhoods of Amsterdam
and was immediately impressed by the courage of her commitment to therapy in difficult clinical situations. Her devotion to
helping was matched by her quick insight into complex relationships; she displayed a natural talent and intuition as a therapist.

I often wondered how ElseMarie's broad background in her
large extended family in Brabant led to her sensitivity to a
radically new therapeutic approach, applicable to families with
the most painfully disrupted patterns. In any case, few people
have shown a more genuine understanding for the long-term
therapeutic leverages of hidden relational integrity among
family members.

This small volume, I believe, accurately presents the ideas and
methods fundamental to Contextual Therapy. Above all, it
reflects the love of and trust in humanity that form the basis
of all therapy.

Ivan Boszormenyi-Nagy, M.D.

PREFACE

The notion of science implies progress. This progressive development is not found in art. Rodin is different from but does not go further than Praxiteles or the artist who carved the bust of Nefretete in the eighteenth dynasty of the Pharaohs.

The art of healing, in particular that of the soul and human relations, is a mixture of artistic skill and knowledge. Is progress evident here? Who can tell? Certainly, contemporary experts readily recognize their own insights in ancient myths.

The most celebrated myth of all is that of Oedipus. In Athens it assumed unforgettable profiles in at least three tragedies of the poet Sophocles. In the Greek legend, Oedipus, who was cast out as a foundling and grew up in a strange land, returns to his native Thebes and kills, on that journey home, his own father . . . "by chance." By chance?

It is this myth particularly which has captivated and driven depth psychology to portray the deadly threat, rivalry and jealousy between successive generations. In every human being there is hidden such an Oedipus, and there are many talented people who feel free only when they think they have pushed, either physically or mentally, their fathers or their mothers out of the center of their existence. That desire is not always clear or clarifying, however, and it is not unjustly that it acquired the name of "complex," or complication.

That which, at the turn of the century, psychiatrists had heard in the privacy of their offices eventually manifested itself in the culture at large. The therapists listened to admissions of the urge

to kill one's father; now we live in a society in which many fathers
are actually missing from the family. Young people seek independence and pleasure, singing the praises of a life-style free
of most constraints. They are suffering because of that. Paradox-
ically, this freedom is itself a constraint—because it blinds
today's Oedipus to his past and takes from him the roots, home,
family, and security which alone can provide inner peace . . .
and freedom.

In his efforts to explain dreams, whims, and unconscious
errors, Freud chose—some would claim too one-sidedly—
certain tales from the treasure trove of ancient myths. Why were
these particular tales chosen? By chance? Psychoanalysts leave
little room for chance in their attempts to unravel other people's
lives. Overlooked, however, in the attention to Oedipus is
another myth concerning father and son, the myth of Aeneas. It
is every bit as Greek as that of Oedipus, though it has been han-
ded down to us principally through the work of the most famous
poet of the Latin world, Virgil.

When Troy is ablaze and on the point of destruction, Aeneas,
one of its great heroes, flees the city with his wife and son, but not
without bearing on his shoulders his aged father, Anchises. Crip-
pled and blinded by the gods, Anchises is a burden even when
not being borne. Yet Aeneas carries him - and on his way to
founding the Empire. Only after his death does Anchises become for Aeneas his most reliable guide in the underworld.

It is not an easy task to bear with aging parents, especially as
they are seldom blameless. But it is perhaps the only way for a
young person to grow up and become a mature human being.
Bearing this burden, rather than casting it off, is the price to be
paid for future freedom, for a life free of complex.

In our society, and in the field of psychiatry particularly, the
Oedipus complex and its doctrine of deadly rivalry and fear of
parents, has been extraordinarily influential in not only explain-
ing but determining our behavior. Some people were freed from
constraints—sometimes on solitary heights, often in lonely
depression.

As we return to the source of our existence, connecting the claims of past and present, we find residing within us a need for loyalty, an invisible motive no less deeply anchored than the impulse toward fighting. I have known personally a number of young people, who had lost all will to live, with families in the background whom they found strange and even, occasionally, repulsive. These young people found a task and a desire to live again by reconciling themselves with their complicated roots and foundations. Reconciliation? Yes, but more than mere reconciliation—rather, by giving these roots their due. Roots from a world of ethics long suppressed begin to sprout. And in the psychic realm—of happiness or sorrow, of belonging or alienation —those sprouts may best flourish. As soon as those young people take up their burden, a heroic Aeneas begins to grow within them.

I owe these intuitions to the lectures and written works of Ivan Boszormenyi-Nagy, a delicate artist in the art of healing family relationships, as well as to the two talented disciples who here follow in his footsteps. Their living language and praxis find expression in this book.

Jan van Kilsdonk, S.J.

INTRODUCTION

This book came about in close cooperation with Ivan Boszormenyi-Nagy. Through our study trips to Philadelphia, through numerous personal conversations, and by means of participating in the yearly seminars Nagy has conducted in Amsterdam for our students and former students, we have been able to follow closely the development of his thinking.

We have tried to acquire his vision in such a way that we may transmit what seem to us the most important facets of his work. Nagy* has coined for his approach the term "Contextual Therapy." "Context" indicates the existence of an ethical dynamic connection between one person and his or her important relationships. Although Nagy is widely known as a family therapist and we write chiefly about families in this introductory book, the term is meant to include both individual and family therapies. For whether one treats an individual or an entire family, the therapeutic contract in this approach always includes those family members who are not present and those of subsequent generations as well. In this sense there is no contradiction between individual and family therapy. The principle of *multidirected partiality,* the ability to side with the interests of each separate person, is always the guideline.

In his Contextual approach, Nagy distinguishes four dimensions of the relational reality of each person:

---

*We refer to Ivan Boszormenyi-Nagy as Nagy throughout this book.

- *The dimension of FACTS.* This aspect of reality is based on the influence which derives from our genetic roots, physical health, and genetic features, as well as from such events as divorce, adoption, disability, unemployment.

- *The dimension of PSYCHOLOGY.* This pertains to basic needs: ego strength, conditioning, defense mechanisms, satisfaction, fantasies, dreams, insight. This dimension is based on the description of motivations within the individual.

- *The dimension of TRANSACTIONS.* This is the domain of patterns of observable behavior and communication between people. Descriptions of transactions include terminology of systems theory and sociology, such as structures, subsystems, rules, feedback mechanisms, role distribution, and power alignments.

- *The dimension of RELATIONAL ETHICS.* This fourth dimension refers to fairness in the relationship, the relational equilibrium, the balance between earned merit and obligations. Concepts such as loyalty, trust, trustworthiness, and entitlement belong to this realm. This dimension considers the strong connection between the influence on the individual of the earnings of *former generations* and how this legacy will be used in the design of his/her life and in influencing *future generations.*

This last dimension will be the most important guideline for the Contextual approach in psychotherapy because, according to Nagy, it is there that the most effective and fundamental results are to be expected. One should never lose sight of the other three dimensions, however; in both diagnosis and therapy, close attention to facts, psychology, and transactional patterns is vital.

The concept of "ethics" in this approach must not be regarded as a moralistic principle, as a "should." In all relationships, there are certain balances of trustworthiness and mutual rights and obligations. There is an ethical dimension rooted not in culture or morality, but in the condition of mutual merit and obligations between people. In view of the relational ethical balance, the core is that the therapist show sincerely his concern for the interests of everyone involved in that relationship.

It follows that, for Nagy, justice is not a juridical concept, but an ethical one. A relationship is fair if there is a fair balance in the giving and receiving of rights and obligations.

Concepts such as justice, fairness, loyalty, and trustworthiness belong to the language of relational ethics; they have received little attention in psychological thinking. Thus, the language to express those concepts in psychological terms is as yet in its inchoate stages; it is still being developed.

Our book concentrates attention on this ethical dimension because we believe that its precepts remain too little known and as yet play an insufficient role in therapy.

The uniqueness of Nagy's approach is that he connects the ethical dimension with all the others. This opens new possibilities for understanding the phenomena of human relationships and, consequently, has far-reaching therapeutic implications.

We have limited ourselves exclusively to interpreting Nagy's vision and resisted the temptation to compare his work with that of other authors.

It is our hope that this book may serve as an introduction to Nagy's work and that the interested readers will find that it makes more accessible a vision that is sometimes complicated, but always fascinating.

Ammy van Heusden & ElseMarie van den Eerenbeemt

1

FROM ORIGIN TO FUTURE: AN INTRODUCTORY CONVERSATION

The following discussion with Ivan Boszormenyi-Nagy focuses on the development of Contextual Therapy and highlights a number of the important aspects of his approach.

Q: You were born in Hungary and moved to America in 1950. Do you think that your personal life has influenced your vision of life and therapy?

IBN: Probably both events have been important. Personally, I think that the main influence has been that even before entering medical school I was deeply interested in helping psychotics. Here were suffering, unfairly suffering, human beings whose condition was a mystery that neither medicine nor psychology had solved. So the challenge was there for me even before medical school.

I began my medical training knowing that I would pursue psychiatry. I grew up in a society which was still closely in touch with the traditional extended family. It was already beginning to change into one reflecting contemporary urban patterns. As a young psychiatrist I was interested in the psychotherapy of psychosis mainly on an existential basis and in the possibilities of research for the sake of expanding knowledge. Early in my work as a psychiatric resident at the University of Budapest in 1945 and 1946, I was influenced by the relationship-oriented thinking of Kalman Gyarfas. Gyarfas never became a family therapist, but he was a deeply sensitive dynamic therapist who always thought in terms of relationships. He lived in Chicago after 1947, and it was there that I worked under him at the Illinois State Psychiatric Institute. Virginia Satir, by the way, also credits him as a mentor.

Q: In your thinking about the significance of existential human relationships, you refer to the philosophy of Mar-

tin Buber concerning "the dialogue." In what way has
Buber influenced your vision of human relations and
therapy?

IBN: Although I have always been interested in existential views
of human relationships and therapy, the greatest influence
on my thinking came somewhere in the mid-fifties from
Martin Buber's writings. I consider Buber's work to be far
ahead of our time. He struggles with an area which has no
real language as yet. In reading his book *I and Thou,** one
can follow him to a point through language, and then, sud-
denly, the requirement is to follow him without language.
His main contribution is the concept of the dialogue,
which is the basic model of all close human relationships.
It is the basis, also, of the therapeutic concept of my approach. His concept of the genuine dialogue describes
relationships as the true definition of the Self. The dialogue
loses its dynamic meaning if the person is not involved
as Self.

   I believe that success in therapy ultimately depends on
catalyzing or evoking a genuine dialogue between a person
and his or her close relationships. I have been more influenced by Buber than by any other author. I think my approach goes beyond him in the way I regard intergenerational relationships in a dialogue framework; this is less
explicit in Buber. One of the main concepts of my approach, the earning of Entitlement, necessarily is a dialec-
tical one because it describes the process of receiving
through giving, through caring about the other. The gain
of personal liberation through relationships is a unique
option that is connected with what Buber describes as a
genuine dialogue.

Q: You consider your approach as an integration of the individual psychoanalytic concepts developed by Freud and

---

*Buber, M. *I and Thou,* 2nd. Rev. Ed. New York: Charles Scribners Sons,
1958.

the concepts of system theory applied to families and groups. Can you explain this to us?

IBN: The various sources of my development as a therapist have, of course, included the psychodynamic framework of Freud and many variations of that, especially the object relations theory of Ronald Fairbairn and the work of the great therapists of schizophrenia in the fifties. I have been in personal contact with many of the prominent therapists of schizophrenia, particularly those from the Chestnut Lodge Sanatorium in Rockville, Maryland.

Later on in the fifties, I was also one of the early developers of family therapy, which was at first associated with general systems theory. Although I have never been a trained psychoanalyst, I have studied the literature thoroughly. My work at Eastern Pennsylvania Psychiatric Institute started in 1957 with a research inpatient service for the therapy of psychosis. Initially, my staff and I did intensive individual therapy, but in 1958 I introduced family therapy in all cases because I became convinced that it was a more parsimonious and more effective method of treatment.

The decision to start family therapy in all cases at my service arose from several experiences and convictions. One was the early influence of the work of Kalman Gyarfas. Another was my interest in applying Fairbairn's object relations theory to a form of relational therapy. Fairbairn was a Scottish psychoanalyst who redesigned all psychoanalytic theory on relational rather than instinctual terms. In addition, as a result of a visit by Maxwell Jones of London, I introduced "therapeutic community" meetings on my service, including once-a-week meetings with all the relatives of the patients. These influences came together in the observation that relationships should form the basis of effective therapeutic design.

Soon after that, I established contact with some other early family therapists: Nathan Ackerman, Murray Bowen,

Lyman Wynne and, later, Carl Whitaker. All early family therapists shared the excitement surrounding the systems point of view. It seemed to explain phenomena beyond the individual psychology level, which had previously been the only basis of psychotherapeutic understanding. Including the family improved our capability to treat psychotics.

Retrospectively, I believe that perhaps an even greater innovation in family therapy was not a new causal explanation, but a new ethic of contracting for therapy, which was itself implicit in seeing families. The ethics of the contract for therapy constitutes a different reason for choosing the family as a unit to work with than a causal analysis of systemic or individual determination. Responsibility for all those who will be affected by his or her work makes the therapist a humanist who stands on firmer ethical—and even legal—ground in therapy.

Even classical individual therapy implies a contract with persons other than the patient because it does affect other lives. Among family therapists, I have been one of those who have been interested in retaining a perspective on the reality that the individual himself also represents a systemic level of his own, being a whole as an existential and psychological unit. It must not be forgotten that relationships are multiple individual fields too. There is a simple individual perspective, then there is a systems perspective, and finally a multiple individual perspective. The individual is not just a psychodynamic system, but also an existential, ethical entity. This is very important.

Q: Helm Stierlin has called your approach a third paradigm next to psychoanalysis and classical family therapy. You have integrated psychoanalytic thinking with systems thinking in an overall dimension of relational ethics. What do you think of this statement?

IBN: I consider that the new paradigm in my approach is the unifying view of the ethical dimension as the basis of relationships. Relational ethics is a human universal which does not depend on particular value systems, but on the fairness of the distribution of merits, benefits and burdens.

Q: What is your place in the field of family therapy and among family therapists?

IBN: During my 42 years of work as a therapist, I have worked with families for some 29 years. How do I see my role in the field? I was among the first to develop a training center, and I have never lost my interest in psychotherapy as a whole. I am concerned about the quality and standards of psychotherapy from the point of view of the consumer. Therefore, I would like to integrate what has been learned from family therapy with all other valuable therapeutic methods for the benefit of the consumer. And here again we come to the importance of my emphasis on ethics. When ethical consideration becomes the main methodology, it also provides the broadest foundation on which to integrate all kinds of techniques. Thus, concern for all people to be affected by therapy becomes a more important issue than who is present in the therapy room.

Q: More specifically, what is the meaning of "ethics" in your approach?

IBN: The level of the ethics or justice of relationships transcends the level of power dynamics. The expectation of equal returns as a basis for reliable relationships is to a great extent governed by the relative power of the parties involved. Whereas in what I call asymmetrical relationships, i.e. those between a parent and a newborn child or an adult and a terminally ill parent, rewards are governed by the ethics of caring rather than by the equality of returns. It is essential, therefore, in family relationships to define what the ethics of asymmetrical relationships are, as distinguished from the symmetry of business and political relationships or of friendships between equals.

Q: In an interview with Margaret Markham in 1981,* you expressed the wish for a real renaissance of values in human relationships. What did you mean by that?

IBN: The term "renaissance of values in human relationships" refers to a new learning that proceeds from the dialectic of the earning of entitlement and what that means for all human relationships between groups. That is, rather than separating selfishness or self-serving interests from noble altruism as the sole alternatives, a third alternative is added—self-gain via due caring. Receiving through giving serves the interest of the Self and becomes a motivational force which differs from self-denying altruism. The important part of this view is the emphasis on the Contextual approach in the consideration of posterity. Posterity is vulnerable and exposed to any input from the present.

Therefore, areas such as education, contraception and planned parenthood, support for new structures of parenting such as single-parent families, regulation of open adoption, child custody, foster care and juvenile court procedures all should be affected by this kind of future-oriented planning. The renaissance in human relationships is extremely concerned with that aspect of modern life which deeply dips into borrowing from the future.

Q: How did the concept of justice originate and develop in your vision?

IBN: I consider the notion of justice as a dynamic of relationships to be the key concept of my book, with Spark, *Invisible Loyalties.*** It came from many years of searching for an understanding of the dynamics of a therapy that would be most beneficial to families and relationships. It derived

---

*Boszormenyi-Nagy, I. Contextual therapy: The realm of the individual: An interview with Margaret Markham. *Psychiatric News,* XVI, 20–21,1981.

**Boszormenyi-Nagy, I. & Spark G.M. *Invisible Loyalties.* New York: Harper & Row, 1973; Brunner/Mazel, 1984.

from the search for a more far-reaching and long-term explanation of why and how relationships can be viable or maintainable, recognizing that observable transactions and communications are only ephemeral manifestations. Relationships and life as a whole have *long-term* programming—much in the way that genes program biological life—not just mechanisms of minute-by-minute survival. In some manner, fairness on a long-term basis constitutes trustworthiness and, therefore, long-term viability of close relationships. Justice as fairness is the foundation of trustworthiness of relationships, which is in itself the foundation of viability. If a relationship is always unilaterally exploitative, if one takes but does not give over a prolonged period of time, then the relationship becomes lastingly unfair, untrustworthy and nonviable. By that I mean that people either leave the relationship or develop signs of strain or pathology.

There is no need to assume that there is a state of lasting justice or an island of justice on earth. What is required instead is periodic monitoring of the degree of fairness or unfairness in one's relationships. One must be responsible for reviewing the occasional, inevitable developing unfairness of any relationship. As long as I care about reviewing and correcting injustices that occur, I satisfy the trustworthiness of the relationship.

Fairness, of course, is not meant to be absolutely equal in terms of mutual expectations since there is an inherent asymmetry of some relationships, such as that between parent and small child. Fairness has a modified meaning here. The child will never be able to give returns in an equitable way to the parent and, in part, will have to return through posterity, whether to his own biological child or to posterity in general. In this sense, justice as fairness is the basis of relational ethics. It is not a value. It is a dynamic balance between the amount of give and take and each person's capacity for returning what was received.

Why is justice such an important dimension in my thinking? It took years of effort as I tried to understand what makes therapy workable with families, what constitutes the essential material with which we work in relationships, what ultimately holds them together when it comes to the point of despair, to the point of psychosis, to the point of suicide. That kind of thinking led me to considering the justice of *give and take.* This means not only justice but also the source of trustworthiness. If the relationship is fair, then I trust it on a basis of reality. It could be that I trust because I am naive or because you gain my trust through clever manipulation, like a swindler. I can be manipulated to trust someone and then be hurt later. A trustworthy relationship is one in which it is appropriate and *right* to trust. This, of course, is related to Martin Buber's notion of justice of the human order or the justice of the order of being. Who determines this justice? Is it entirely subjective? Are your values—or the father's values or the son's values—needed to determine other people's justice?

The justice of the human order is not kept in any court. It is being worked on in the dialogue between two people, each of whom tries honestly to make his own side clear and to some extent hears the other's side, too. In that interaction they mutually define where trustworthiness lies. So, in that sense, it is neither subjective nor objective, but certainly it is not dependent on values. It depends on the reality of give and take between persons.

Q: In this book there is emphasis on Loyalty, Trust and Entitlement. Can you point out some connections between these concepts?

IBN: Of course they are related. It is trustworthiness that counts here as a relational concept rather than trust, but of course trust can be maintained only in a trustworthy relation of prolonged duration. So we all have a need for being able to trust. But we are not right to trust if the relationship is not trustworthy.

The loyalty concept is a broader one. Loyalty is also based on earned merit. So in that sense I am loyal to my family of origin because I have received so much from them. Loyalty is a triadic or triangular concept in the sense that it is much more than just an attachment. I think it includes the option to be loyal either to you or to someone else. If I am loyal to you, I am not loyal to someone else. So it involves the choice of attachment. It is examplified, for instance, in the loyalty conflict concept, where vertical (parents and child) and horizontal (or peer type) relationships compete with each other. So one is either loyal or disloyal to the vertical expectation of loyalty.

The trustworthy person has earned entitlement. In return, he deserves loyalty or some extra credit, extended beyond the moment-by-moment give and take—beyond the expedience of the moment. I give an extra consideration to my parents because they have earned entitlement. I should be loyal to them because of what they have contributed to me in the past.

Q: What are necessary conditions for the therapist to be able to use your approach and what are the most important items for a training program?

IBN: The therapist will have many difficulties in learning the approach because of the great demands upon a flexible open-mindedness regarding the giving up of prejudicial thinking. That is probably the greatest difficulty. We are all conditioned to a certain kind of prejudicial thinking from early childhood. It is even part of our loyalty to our own group. The other group is considered as bad and our group as good. To overcome these prejudices in one's personal and professional life so as to become multilaterally fair places a great demand on the therapist. Not all will succeed in handling it. People come and go in that regard. Therefore, in training programs, it is very important to connect the work on one's own family with these principles so that students are able to learn from their teacher or supervisor the application of this multilaterality not only to the families with whom they are working but to their own relationships as well.

Q: How does your therapeutic approach provide a connection between healing and prevention?

IBN: As far as healing and prevention are concerned, I think that the consequences of this approach for the future are so evident that we cannot help but accomplish some kind of prevention. This is true in individual therapy as well, for it, too, affects the next generation. It is just that the individual therapist does not care about or is unable to see the outcome. The family therapist is generally better able to see some of the effects of relationships on children. Or he is more curious to find out about what affected the child who has grown up. He is better able to determine retrospectively what has led to the present consequences. If the therapist completely closes himself to intergenerational issues and works exclusively with couples therapy, then of course his awareness of consequences is circumscribed.

Q: What is your vision of the future of the family?

IBN: The future of the family? I don't know. I think there is a tremendous disintegration of reliability and of the capacity for maintaining relationships in a close sense. At the same time, the parent-child relationship has to be supported. Here the difficulty again is that the long-term implications of neglectful parenting are not easily seen. It is our job as therapists to explore them and make society more aware of them.

Q: What influence do you expect the feminist movements to have on society?

IBN: I think feminist movements are understandable because women had to carry a great deal of the additional burdens as the extended family disintegrated. They had to provide security as mothers, even though they had lost supporting relationships; that is no small burden. I understand the anger of the feminist woman. On the other hand, I hope that in the long run it will lead to a better understanding between the sexes. Women are, by nature, specialists in close relationships because of the fact that they have to go through pregnancy and breastfeeding, their biological capabilities. They can be teachers and leaders in helping men to participate more fully in close relationships. The ultimate goal is to strengthen the parenting team.

Q: Which developments in society do you believe most important for human relationships and for the individual?

IBN: Society should design agencies and services to provide support for parenting. We should help to introduce the new dialectic of the earning of entitlement into public understanding. There is too much of a separation between the two extremes of "Either I serve my own interest or I get ripped off." There is no middle ground in most business or political relationships, yet there must be. This is what the idea of entitlement can provide. Gradually, the model of the self-reinforcing motivation of the earning of entitlement via caring should be introduced into public awareness. The hope for the future is that individuals will be able to connect self-gain with consideration for others.

2
LOYALTY

Loyalty Between Parents and Children

Before one can fully understand the nature of relationships in the nuclear and extended family, one must first understand the essence of the concept of loyalty that is involved here.

Unlike the loyalty associated with religion, national interest, and group interest, this concept refers to "ontic" loyalty that has a real existence rather than to feelings of loyalty. The roots of this ontic loyalty are grounded in the origin of existential, asymmetrical ties between parent and child. At birth, every human being begins an undeniable, irreversible relationship with his or her parents, a relationship based upon biological, hereditary kinship and fortified by joint possession in the inheritance of the assets and liabilities of previous family generations as well as personal legacies, expectations, and unwritten *laws* within kinships. In fact, the etymology of the word "loyalty" refers to the French word for law: *Loi.*

Throughout the generations, these original parent-child loyalties are imbedded in a nurturing soil whose nature and quality are formed by the amount of trust, merits, and justice built in the course of ages.

The joint possession of loyalty roots and of inheritance built by former generations shapes an irreplaceable bond between people. This bond is not only able to resist physical and geographical separation but also determines the degree to which the offspring feels free—as a result of the original resources of trust—to engage in new relationships outside the domain of the families of origin.

People remain loyal to their families of origin long after they have, by choice, or necessity, broken their bonds with them. The primary bond of loyalty between parent and child, the ability to be available and to give, influences powerfully every human

17

being's attitude towards the world outside the family of origin. The loyalty tie to the origin sets invisible forces in motion so that one is often not conscious of remaining loyal to one's origin even while making the choices and decisions regarding relationships established with other people.

Loyalty, therefore, is a fundamental force in the formation of the individual. In this concept of acknowledging and recognizing loyalty bonds, the adult individual becomes an autonomous person specifically by rendering an account of the existence of loyalty bonds and by integrating this notion actively in his or her design of life. Loyalty is fundamentally bound to the existential fact that every human being has come into existence through his parents. For the parents, the existential fact is that their children are born out of them. In the latter instance, the human being starts as a totally dependent creature. The fact that the mother has nurtured the child within herself and then given birth places every grown child under an existential indebtedness to his or her mother. In this regard, the father has arrears at the time of the birth. When the father assumes the consequences and the responsibility of parenthood, the child comes into another equally indebted existential relationship.

As long as the human being lives, he remains connected with his origins. Whatever events may have transpired since the birth of a child, the loyalty of the child to his parents remains.

> Peter, 16 years, is in residential treatment: "I had a miserable childhood. My mother was a bitch. She drank and she neglected me. But at school I was always getting into fights with anyone who said anything against her."

Even in case of adoption immediately after birth, the justified claim of the child to the origin of his existence remains. If the adoptive parents acknowledge and integrate this fact into their relationship with the child, both the adoptive parents and the child will benefit. Loyaly is, in this approach, the existential context of everyone who is born. (We will return later in this chapter to the subject of adoption.)

Loyalty expresses itself and receives its shape in a relational ethical context. In this context, the original trust, the mutuality of give and take between parents and child, the indebtedness and obligation to each other, and the personal responsibility become the building blocks for the development of the child.

The concept of "loyalty" has in this framework nothing to do with a normative principle by which one "should" be loyal. It would be a misunderstanding of the concept if one thought that the more one is loyal to his origin, the better it will be for his personal growth. The contrary can be the case. One can feel over-loyal to one's parents and, as a result, experience excessive pressure to be obliged to them, suffering seriously in the long run. If the loyalty of the child is exploited and misused, the reserve of trust, which is present in each human being, will be continually depleted.

In other instances, one can be caught in a web of destructive invisible loyalties. It is then of utter importance to strip oneself of this constraint.

Vertical Versus Horizontal Loyalty

Between the continuously succeeding generations are imbedded the *vertical* bonds of loyalty: the asymmetrical, irreversible relationship between parents and child. Inevitably in life, new relationships come into being: One gains brothers and sisters, friendships develop, marriages are contracted; some relationships end, others last a lifetime.

Those relationships in which the partners are in an equal position, characterized by mutual rights and obligations, shape the *horizontal* loyalties. These loyalties lack the irreversible characteristics of the parent-child relationship. When the vertical loyalties cross the horizontal loyalties, an option of choice arises. At such a moment, one chooses consciously or unconsciously in favor of a certain relationship. Do I remain loyal to my parents or do I declare my loyalty for another? In such a situation, one affirms priorities: One relationship is chosen over the other. In family relationships, one is not loyal on the basis of power, but on the basis of acquired merits. What matters is the balance of mutual justice and merits, not loyalty based on emotional factors.

Balance in Movement

In the course of each person's life the vertical and horizontal loyalties will cross each other again and again. It is through this process that one can develop the ability to balance old and new loyalty bonds and gain the freedom to engage in new relationships. In the following transitional phases especially, a new equilibrium has to be established:

> birth
> growing up
> adulthood
> partnership-marriage
> parenthood
> grandparenthood
> loss (death) of parents

New relationships carry new expectations and obligations. Both partners must deal with their vertical loyalties. Vertical and horizontal loyalties inevitably come into confrontation with each other and evoke conflicts; this is the reality of life. Such confrontations are common, human phenomena, entirely acceptable. Within the formations of one's own adult conditions, one must find an equilibrium if one is to be appropriately loyal. It is an equilibrium gained only through continual examination of one's relationships.

In spite of the fact that they are deeply rooted and have the color of blood, vertical loyalty bonds are often denied or minimized. Cutting, avoiding, denying or damaging these bonds of loyalty can often undermine the formation of new relationships. In that case, the vital sources deliver too little oxygen. If one imagines the vertical and horizontal loyalties as a ladder, then the uprights no longer support the rungs, and the ladder breaks down each time at the same spot, the junction. As stated previously, every relationship can be ended except that between parent and children.

At the time of the birth of children, who will carry on the asymmetry in the vertical line, a new bond develops between grandparents, parents, and children; one often sees a change in the manner the adults relate to each other, a change engendered by the new life. Grandparents, who are less tense and without the pressure that attends the responsibility of raising the children themselves, can be milder than the parents in their relationships with the children. Interestingly, this often improves the relationship with their own children and the grandchildren themselves will also make an effort to improve the relationship between their parents and grandparents.

> A six-year-old girl, Trudy, put on her list of wishes for her birthday this most cherished one: "Grandpa and Grandma should come to visit my birthday party." The relationship with the grandparents had been cut off for years. Trudy's parents reacted with astonishment and anger. The existence of the grandparents had not been mentioned for years.

The aging process and eventual death of one of the grandparents and the connected mourning can cause a radical shift in the loyalty management.

> In one family the problems within the marriages of three daughters became visible only after the death of the father, a warm patriarch. The choice of their partners and the relationships with them had been grafted upon the relationship with the father, which had been strong and had remained important, significant, throughout their adult years. His death placed great pressure on the horizontal bonds of the daughters and their spouses; eventually the relationships could not stand the stress.

The manner of dealing with the death of one of the parents and the permission or the prohibition to mourn are often deter-

mined throughout the generations. The prohibition to mourn
has serious implications for the marital relationship. When
someone is not allowed by his or her partner to mourn the loss of
a parent, the account will, eventually, be charged against the
partner, sometimes even resulting in that partner's being
deserted.

Even a whole family can unconsciously conspire in its effort to
prohibit the family members their mourning process. The result
of this effort will be a standstill in the emotional growth of every
family member. The unconscious collusion plays an important
role in the development of serious difficulties in the relationships within the family. On the other hand, if room exists for understanding and sympathy, relationships will be strengthened.

Loyalty Conflicts

Loyalty conflicts become unlivable when the tension reaches a
point where it hinders one's capacity to be loyal to his or her vertical relationships. Vertical loyalty bonds are deeply rooted in
spite of their often being denied or minimized. If one cannot be
openly loyal to one's origins, those bonds will seek less visible
routes, like blood that will stream to its destination via all kinds of
alternate vessels. A Dutch proverb expresses this clearly: "The
blood creeps where it cannot flow."

Horizontal (chosen) relationships will be seriously impaired
by cutting off, avoiding, or denying vertical loyalties. Loyalty
conflicts are tangible and inherent in everyone's life. Every important choice in life carries with it a shifting within the loyalty
system. The real meaning of autonomy and freedom proceeds
from the discovery of an equilibrium within one's own adult
conditions. This equilibrium represents a balance in movement.

Invisible Loyalties

When tension arises from a person's inability to be openly loyal
to his origin, the loyalties become invisible because they have to
be denied. These invisible loyalties exert a powerful influence

over the optional, chosen relationship; they impede or preclude the chance for mutuality within a peer relationship—sometimes to the extent of that relationship's complete stagnation.

> A couple married for 10 years requested therapeutic help. Their marriage had been severely jolted when it was revealed that the wife had, for a year, engaged in extramarital affairs of short duration. The father of this woman had died a year and a half before. On his deathbed he had confessed to his daughter that he regretted his strict, fundamental matrimonial ethic. He asked her if she had noticed the tension in the marriage of her parents. Although she had almost certainly noticed it, she denied it to her dying father and decided to keep this last conversation with him a secret from her mother.

The invisible loyalty towards parents or previous generations continues to influence one's behavior towards innocent and unwitting third parties (chosen relationships). One's invisible loyalty relationships pertain to the positive or negative outcome of the balance of merits, obligations, and trustworthiness of generations, and one is often unconscious of their influence and expression.

> A 24-year-old woman had become a mother but felt unable to care for her child. She was aggressive towards her baby (postnatal depression). It appeared that a serious impairment existed in the mother-daughter relationship of the mother and her grandmother. When, after therapeutic help, the mother-as-daughter was able to restore active loyalties toward the grandmother, it followed that, in turn, she was capable of being a mother to her child; her depression disappeared.

Through this restored open loyalty toward her own mother, achieved by repairing the rupture in the primary loyalty, the mother obtained the right and freedom to be a mother herself.

In the case of asymmetrical, vertical bonds, there are often three generations with coinciding or conflicting interests from which must be effected a balance of entitlements and obligations. Had therapeutic help failed, the innocent baby in the above example would have been presented with the unfair account of the impaired equilibrium between generations.

Adulthood and Loyalty

The growth or growing up of any member of the family carries with it shifts and changes in the loyalty fabric. The forces of the loyalty system often remain hidden, but the effects may appear at the onset of a new phase of life, as when someone leaves the family. Relinquishing or letting go of the exclusivity of the family of origin and devoting oneself to friendships, romantic relationships, and marriage require a basic trust from which new rights, expectations, and obligations can be formed.

However, in some families every movement toward the autonomy of the child is considered an act of disloyalty. Remaining at home is openly disapproved of, but covertly appreciated as evidence of loyalty to the family of origin. Many adults living independently still function as children and remain intensively linked with their parents. The reluctance or inability to enter into another relationship (such as marriage) may result from this state of complete availability to the parents (overloyalty).

> A 30-year-old woman with agoraphobia claims, "I cannot leave home in a normal manner; I could break away only with violence. I will remain at home until my parents die."

The parents of this woman maintained that their daughter had no obligation towards them, that they did not want anything from her, and, furthermore, that they could not accept anything from her. This resulted in the daughter's sense of total obligation and indebtedness to her parents.

Because of this nonreceiving attitude, her development was seriously impaired. She could not engage in new relationships, but remained fearful and full of blame and resentment toward her parents. On the other hand, a unilateral cutting of relationships, a breaking away from the family of origin, can, during the process of an adolescent's disengagement, lead to the same lack of freedom as in the above example.

> Peter, a 19-year-old boy from a strict religious environment, breaks away radically from his parents to join a fanatic sect in which he imposes upon himself a new set of equally severe restrictions.

The more rigid the bonds of an adolescent with his family of origin, the harder it will be for him to feel free in a chosen relationship. This is in contrast with the prescriptions of society which claim that a rupture with the family of origin is often a normal step in the direction of autonomy.

Delinquency

A juvenile delinquent may seem the cause of disruption in the family, but often he is, on the contrary, loyal in a special way. By his delinquent behavior the child protects his parents from the pain of their disturbed marital relationship; he diverts the disturbance onto himself. If the child is institutionalized or hospitalized on a psychiatric ward, the guilt of the excluded child increases: He feels that he is no longer able to be loyal to his family of origin and often this is indeed made impossible for him.

If the family is not engaged in the treatment plan, the family may fail to acknowledge the child's side of justice and entitlement. As a result, the child often selects another child as a target for scapegoating and victimizing. He releases his pent-up rage toward the outside world and exonerates thereby the image of his parents. As he pushes the outside world down, the parents "rise."

Phenomena such as delinquency and drug addiction can be investigated in terms of the underlying loyalties within the intergenerational balances of justice and injustice. In fact, the outside world has to pay (receives the revolving slate of) the unsettled accounts.

Incest and Loyalty

The trust of a child, his loyalty, and his need to please his parents can be easily exploited. The child wants to be loyal even while he is exploited and misused. The resources of trust—present in everyone by the asymmetry at the time of the birth—are continuously depleted. In the case of incest, the life history is often one beset with secrets and shame.

In incest situations, the most important single issue facing the therapist is that of respecting family trust reserves. People may prefer to terminate treatment entirely rather than betray their fundamental loyalties. The acknowledgment of this deep underlying concern for the members of the family will grant the freedom to converse. One has to consider continuously the potential trust resources within the loyalty system and preserve for the parent his or her adult responsibilities.

It often turns out that the parents themselves have been emotionally neglected as children, and, in many cases, physically or sexually abused. The therapist must acknowledge that. This discovery does not diminish parental responsibilities, but here the parents are not excluded, and the child is not urged to betray his fundamental loyalties.

> Eugene, age 15 is arrested for rape. Prolonged interrogation by the public prosecutor leads him to confess in tears that he has had sexual intercourse with his mother several times. The following day two events occur: Eugene attempts suicide and his mother, who on request of the prosecutor

was informed of her son's confession, runs into a bus, suffering serious injury.

The Ledger and the Revolving Slate

The newborn child gets a place of his own in the ledger of merits and obligations, the intergenerational balance of justice. Every generation passes on to the next generation part of what has been received from the previous one. One is inclined to restore in the next generation what has been out of balance in the previous generation—one tries to be a better parent. When grandparents and parents have unsettled accounts, the child will become involved as well. Unpaid accounts are inherent in life. In the case of serious stagnation in the vertical line, a bill can be transferred to a new account—for instance, a child's account. There is the Dutch saying: "the child of the account" (a child who has to pay the "piper").

The account, which is valid between the parties where it should be settled, is now forwarded to an innocent third party in an unjust manner. These revolving slates disturb one's own family life, because one has not been able to solve the conflicts of the previous generation.

Liberation from this constantly recurring circle of destructive actions is possible only if one seeks rejunction, and one must sometimes walk a long and painful road to discover which accounts have been unjustly attributed to the present generation. The deceased ancestors should also be included in this process of rejunction; it may be the only way to achieve reconciliation. Note that this "crusade" should not be undertaken as a noble, altruistic mission; the ultimate purpose is rather a liberating gain for all the people at issue. It may seem a paradox, but individuation can be reached most precisely by learning a new balance of relating to one's family of origin. By doing so, one gains entitlement, which enhances one's ability to succeed in other relationships—as a spouse, as a parent.

Marriage, Partnership and Loyalty

> A pair of star-cross'd lovers take their life;
> Whose misadventured piteous overthrows
> Do with their death bury their parents' strife

Shakespeare: Prologue to Romeo and Juliet

Conflicts and problems often arise from hidden loyalties toward the parents. A full understanding of marital problems may depend upon the therapist's ability to trace the development of all loyalty conflicts existing in the household. Marriage* to a partner of a different religious background or ethnic group can constitute rebellion against the family of origin. As the parents reject their offspring's marriage, the offspring may disclaim any loyalty to the family of origin, yet an invisible filial loyalty may reveal itself through the offspring's inadvertent undermining of his or her own marriage.

A good relationship with the in-laws and a poor relationship with one's own family can create an intrinsically dangerous situation for the marriage, especially when someone severs his original relationships.

When one of the parents with whom the rupture had taken place dies, the horizontal relationship receives increased pressure and the account of this disloyalty is increasingly lodged against the partner.

> A man had, with support of his wife, rejected his parents and accepted his parents-in-law as his own. Half a year after the death of his mother, serious marital problems became manifest and he refused to so much as visit his parents-in-law.

Marriage often leads to a confrontation with original loyalties. Without equilibrium, these loyalties will disrupt the marital

---

*We will use the word "marriage" to indicate all forms of partnership.

relationship. The manifestation of the original problem is only the tip of the iceberg.

> A middle-aged man is seriously depressed and suffers from sleeplessness. "I am terribly involved in the problems of my second marriage. I never see the children of my first marriage. Years ago I cut off all contact with my parents— they were worthless, rotten people. I had to do it to live freely".

Marriage has its best chance for mutuality and justice in the balance of give and take when the original loyalty systems of both partners are respected and acknowledged and both spouses are supportive of each other in this matter.

Problems of fairness, justice, and loyalty can never be solved forever. Each of the partners will from time to time resort, unavoidably, to abandoning or denying the interests of the other. But if the mutual concern for each other's interests in regard to the original loyalties dissipates or if the denial of these interests becomes the only way of dealing with loyalty conflicts, then the marriage is seriously threatened.

Successive Generations

Each individual is born into a configuration of previous and current relationships which form the nature of future relationships, a configuration which may determine whether or not one will beget children of one's own. The problems which so often accompany this choice, in which partners can be imprisoned for years, may be the result of loyalty conflicts. What may seem on the surface to be merely a power struggle between the partners is in fact an entanglement rooted in three generations.

The decision not to bear children may be an act of invisible loyalty to the family of origin: One does not allow oneself new binds so that one may remain totally available for the parents. Parentification often underlies this; one is a parent for the parents. By remaining available to care for them, without acknowledging this, one can continue indefinitely and seriously impair the chances of becoming a parent oneself. A child growing up with a heritage of split loyalties will have an image of the surrounding world as untrustworthy. It often seems that one stops the reproduction cycle at the third generation so as not to burden the next generation with this legacy.

> A woman recognized too many similarities between herself and her mother and grandmother. Both had abandoned their spouses early in their marriages and had told their daughters during childhood how detestable their fathers had been. This woman consequently feared to become a mother. She did not want to give her child the pain that had been given to her.

The rights and interests of the unborn child must play an essential role in the decision whether or not to bear children. The woman, who must decide whether to complete her pregnancy or to interrupt it, can be aided in her decision by considering the inherent entitlement of the child: What can she as a mother offer the child? Are the reservoirs of trust sufficient to sustain the child's well-being? A decision which considers the interests and rights of everyone involved, including those of the still unborn child, is the only truly just decision.

Divorce and the Loyalty of the Children Involved

In many divorce cases the demand made on the child is heavy and emotionally loaded, and children may respond to it rejunctively so as to bring about a reunion, as in the following example:

> Rose, age six, said to her father: "If you want to take me with you, I remain with mama; if she wants to take me with her, then I stay with you."

Children forced to choose between their parents are in an impossible and dangerous position; a child will not and cannot choose. A child may be asked in court for his or her opinion but should never be saddled with the unbearably heavy burden of having to choose between parents; he or she must not be designated the decision-maker.

Moreover, the question posed to the child should be formulated in such a way that the child is not placed in the position of being disloyal to either parent.

> Paul, age 11, was asked to choose between living with his father or remaining with his mother. He cut his Snoopy dog—his transitional object—in half and offered each of his parents a piece and said: "This is the way you would like it with me too."

Considering the many implications which a divorce has for parents as it does for children, the loyalty of the child towards *both* parents is of central and vital interest and must be respected. Out of this loyalty, each child can help, especially when there are major conflicts between the parents, to diminish the pain of the conflict. Children find their own ways to console their parents, and it is important that the children receive from their parents some form of acknowledgment for their efforts.

In deciding custody, the court should consider which parent will be more willing and able to sustain the child in his relationship with the other parent and with the latter's relatives. It should search for flexibility and equilibrium rather than adhering to rigid, absolute principles of custodial fitness.

Opportunities for ex-partners to remain a parental team—after the greatest tension and aggression have ebbed away—should be sought and exploited. Ideally, the parental team can maintain or regain a position of trustworthiness in regards to the child. It is vital that the child acknowledge that neither parent can ever be replaced. Indeed, most children strive to continue relationships with both natural parents.

Split Loyalty

A child is caught in a primary split loyalty if the parents present expectations so mutually conflicting that the child can be loyal toward one parent only at the cost of disloyalty toward the other. In contrast with a loyalty conflict, which involves an incompatibility between the vertical loyalty and a horizontal loyalty, split loyalty constitutes a serious crack in the basic trustworthiness between parents and child.

The predicament of split loyalty does not primarily concern a conflict between the parents themselves or even the possibility of divorce. The fact that a child is more involved with one parent than with the other does not necessarily create anxiety. What does cause split loyalty is the child's unavoidable involvement in the rupture of trust between the parents. Torn, the child will endeavor on all levels to be rejunctive between the parents. But the child has been given an impossible task. All his efforts are in vain, and yet he will not give up. He will, for instance, desperately employ all kinds of symptoms as signals to reunite the parents. Nagy offers the following illustration:

> A girl with anorexia nervosa reported a dream in which her parents were dying and lying next to each other in two graves. The time given to the care of one parent could be spent only at the risk of the other's dying.

The child is caught in a split loyalty if the mother and her parents turn against the father and his family and expect and even require that the child do the same. In this way, the child is forced into being loyal toward one parent at the expense of his loyalty to the other. The child will not give up his involvement with his father, but he is presented with a dilemma: "Which side should I choose?" It is a question that cannot be solved by the child. The only way to escape the dilemma is to assume an attitude of indifference since any resolution would mean a costly loss. Thirty years later, when the father is dead and the mother suffers from an illness, the answer of the now grown-up child may be, "I don't care." This is a means of balancing the loyalties through punishing the last surviving parent.

Another consequence may be a paralyzingly ambivalent attitude towards the spouse or the children as the influence of split loyalty extends itself to future generations; the legacy of split loyalty continues in the asymmetrical lines.

The confusion of the child, caused by his inability to effect a rejunction of the parents and the expectation that he will split his loyalty, can lead to the most intense tensions. Split loyalty underlies many suicide attempts and many suicides.

> A mother and her three daughters were linked to each other by their hatred of spouse and father. The oldest daughter attempted suicide. Seriously ill and hospitalized, she asked the nurse to notify her father. When he came to visit her, she said, "There was no other way for me to show mother that you cared, that you, too, would feel sorrow by my death."

When working with the potentially suicidal, it is vital that the therapist not emphasize the estrangement between the parents and their child, but rather focus on the rejunctive principle: "How did you help your parents when there was great trouble between them?" There should be a search for moments in the life of the child when both parents were involved with the child. Helping to search for these moments of shared concern is in itself a rejunctive action.

A suicide attempt may be the ultimate effort to resolve split loyalties, and any indication of suicidal tendencies requires an immediate investigation to determine whether or not an underlying substructure of split loyalties does in fact exist.

Adoption and Loyalty*

Loyalty of children towards their parents stems from facts of conception, birth, and growth. In a modified way the legacy of

---

*This section, broadly applied, includes foster families, as well.

parent-child loyalty remains even when children are given up for adoption or relinquished by the parents at an early phase of life. Whatever has been the nature of the parental responsibility or parental behavior after the birth of the child, the uniqueness of the relationship remains an undeniable fact of life, even if the child has been cast off. And this relationship remains in force even when the separation resulted from the parents' inability to raise the child or from neglect or ill-treatment. The separation itself will be traumatic at several levels and over the course of years.

Children given up for adoption have to deal with their primary loyalty toward their origin and their acquired and merited loyalty toward their adoptive parents and family. The well-being of the child requires the freedom to explore the foundations of her existence; the adoptive parents must never deny the origins of the adoptive child, or deny her right to learn more of her natural parents. Of vital importance for all concerned is that the adoptive parents do not blame or vilify the natural parents.

It may seem paradoxical, but loyalty to the adoptive parents will benefit from their consideration for the child's justified claim to his or her roots.

> An adoptive mother presented this examplary instance of acknowledgment, which was of vital importance to her son: "I am, from the bottom of my heart, grateful to the woman who carried you and gave you birth. She has given us a son and, by doing so, she has been of great importance in your and our history".

Adopted children will be inclined to weave a myth around the real parents. In this unreal wish is embedded the hope that their parents were *forced* to relinquish their child against their inclination to give love and trust. The natural parents become good people with whom the child shares mysterious bonds of loyalty. The adopted child sometimes needs a lifetime to learn how to balance the myth of the superiority of his natural parents with the reality of his loyalty and obligations toward his adoptive parents.

A 25-year-old woman expecting her first child claimed: "I have always believed that I was stolen away from my parents, who were, in my fantasies, beautiful and rich. During adolescence, in a difficult phase with my adoptive parents, I clung to this idea and hoped that my story would come true. I often accused my adoptive parents of narrow-mindedness, and they suffered in comparison with my fantasized vision of my real parents. Now that I am pregnant myself, I understand what it means to be a mother and I feel closer to the woman who carried me. But I find, too, that it has become easier for me to give of myself to my adoptive parents. I know that these are the only grandparents my child will have—and I want them to be real grandparents, not fantasized ones."

Through this newly realized capacity to give to both sides, this woman is able to diminish the either/or polarization, one characteristic of the predicament of split loyalty.

In a special phase of detachment from their adoptive parents, adolescents often institute an inquiry into their lost and unknown parents. They are searching for their identity. This can be viewed as the normal step of an adolescent who rebels against his parents in the process of detachment, but can be an especially difficult phase for the adoptive parents who until then have maintained by secrecy the myth about the natural parents. In contrast to the conditions of a "normal" family, in which rebellion against the parents is less threatening, adoptive parents can be hurt deeply by the child's desire to investigate the truth about her natural parents.

A 39-year-old man, following the death of the last living foster parent, said: "I have waited since I was 18 to start this investigation; I could not do so previously because of the pain it would have caused my foster parents. They would not have been able to cope with it. 'Why my boy, we are your parents!' they'd say. And they were very good to me."

Here it appears that the search for the natural parents was seen as an act of disloyalty toward the adoptive parents, a disregard for their devotion and care. The fear of this is understandable and it requires appropriate help.

In sight of what they consider desertion, adoptive parents prefer secrecy, withholding data, and, occasionally, insinuations about the natural parents.

> An adoptive mother tells her troublesome 15-year-old daughter: "I'd better tell you now, your mother was a fallen, low woman, absolutely wicked, and you should thank the Lord on your bare knees that you were placed with us. Maybe you can understand better now why I am so strict with you. Remember, the apple doesn't fall far from the trunk."

As a result of the sharp contrast—the natural parent is bad, the adoptive parent good—the child enters an unavoidable conflict with his vertical loyalty. It requires courage and love on the part of the adoptive parents for them to talk openly about these matters with the child from an attitude of trust, not of anxiety which fears decreased loyalty and love. In broaching these subjects, the parent should choose carefully both the time and manner most amenable for the child to digest the facts concerning his origin and integrate these in his design of life.

If serious conflicts emerge between the different loyalties and if professional help is requested, both loyalties should be kept in view. The adoptive parents, the natural parents, and the children all carry the burden and feel the weight of the loyalty conflict; the therapeutic strategy should be directed to the interests of all parties. When other common conflicts or tensions arise in the family of the adoptive parents, it is apparent that the adopted child is especially vulnerable and anxious. Often this child volunteers as the family scapegoat, an action that may manifest itself in wayward behavior such as drug and alcohol abuse.

Adoption of children from other cultures requires particularly careful consideration.

> A seven-year-old Korean girl adopted by a Dutch family keeps a small suitcase with the clothes which she carried with her when she arrived from Korea. Now and again, when the children in school call her names, she takes her suitcase to the classroom and exhibits her possessions, saying, "I got this from my mother, it was all she had. She gave it to me so that I cannot forget her."

When the foster family and the natural family can cooperate— which requires courage and prudence from both sides—the joint effort can contribute enormously to the healthy development of the child.

> Marciano, a five-year-old boy of Surinam descent, has lived in a Dutch foster family since the death of his mother when he was two years old. Hospitalized by a sudden, serious illness, he was diagnosed as epileptic. His grandmother, who also lived in Holland, was informed of the illness by the foster parents.
>
> When she came to visit, she brought with her a small paper bag with some kind of white powder which she had ordered specially from Surinam. The grandmother explained to Marciano and his foster parents that this powder could exorcise the evil spirits from his body. The foster parents had a moment of hesitation, each out of different considerations, but allowed the grandmother to administer her medicine to the boy. Sometime later, a new examination revealed no traces of epilepsy. When Marciano heard that he no longer needed to take medicine, it was obviously according to his expectations: "Granny and you together have made me better," he told his foster parents.

The crucial task for adoptive and foster parents, as for all parents, is not only to raise children to be healthy adults, but to help them become adults who will themselves be good parents and raise healthy children. Herein the vital interests of parents, children, and grandchildren coincide.

Inheriting a Future

Our heritage is comprised of the benefits and burdens of our past. Our roots contain certain facts passed on through the generations. These facts are of a multiple nature. Some existential facts are fixed. Everyone born is of either the feminine or masculine gender and has a certain color of skin, race, and natural disposition; one is not free to choose. Events such as divorce and adoption, war and oppression, leave imprints of a different sort.

The way in which every human being integrates these conditions, both benefits and burdens, into his design of life, linking himself to future generations, forms his legacy. Within this individual legacy, one already has two streams of influence—from the mother's side and from the father's. Directing the two streams into one smooth confluence can be arduous, but ignoring or denying either part of one's origin can impede not only the course of one's own liberation but also the lifestreams of generations to come. When one acknowledges one's source and assimilates the nourishment it provides, he or she gains personal freedom and bequeaths a legacy of freedom to offspring.

> A man had kept secret from his wife and children his Indonesian descent on his grandmother's and mother's side. As a gift for his retirement, he requested a trip to Indonesia. Immediately attracted to and deeply impressed by the country, he devoted the rest of his life to working with welfare institutions in Java and even changed his will to include as a beneficiary a children's home in Djakarta.

The burdens accumulated through our heritage can weigh upon us through the course of many generations. Every family member has to find a balance in his or her legacy in order to transform guilt, shame, victimization, and split loyalty into personal freedom and relational responsibility, serving thereby the interests of future generations as well.

> Her parents and grandparents killed during the war, a middle-aged Jewish woman was raised in a Catholic environment where she had been left as an infant, her Jewish identity denied throughout her childhood for her own safety. She married in the Catholic church. She longed for a child, but when she finally gave birth to a son, she became seriously depressed and complained of phobias. She refused to feed her child and threatened suicide.
>
> With therapeutic help, she was indoctrinated slowly in Jewish history and culture. She changed back to the Jewish name given her by her parents and her son was circumcised. She volunteered one day a week to cooperate in the upkeep of the Jewish cemetery.
>
> She received great support and strength from her husband, who respected her efforts and realized their importance. He was at her side whenever needed. From the child's point of view, as well, the involvement of both parents with the legacy of the mother proved significant. It promoted freedom and health.

The reestablishment and experiencing of one's personal legacy can contribute to the attainment of individual freedom while simultaneously creating vital resources for society, for it is here that one earns the entitlement to be passed on to future generations.

3
ENTITLEMENT

Trust and Trustworthiness

From his concept of *justice* Nagy has developed the concepts of *trustworthiness* and *merited trust,* which today constitute two cornerstones of Contextual Therapy.

No one is an isolated being standing alone in the center of his own universe; there is always some interaction between that person and the outside world. The quality of the relationships which are established in this interaction determines that person's well-being. Relationships provide opportunities to give as well as to receive. The consideration of each other's interests is of fundamental importance in creating a trustworthy relationship. If a person takes into account his own interests as well as the interests of the other and in that way establishes an equilibrium of mutual interests, he earns merit and is entitled to the acknowledgment of the other.

In our society, which places such emphasis upon competition, it is a widespread belief that one can obtain more for oneself only by depriving the other. The psychotherapeutic schools which emphasize assertiveness for oneself do not place sufficient value upon the interests of the other. The fact that relationships provide possibilities to earn trust and the resulting entitlement transcends the antithesis of seeking profit for oneself versus caring for the interests of others. The process of earning entitlement bridges the gap between egotism and altruism.

In the process of locating one's own and someone else's interests, a positive spiral can be set into motion and lead to the development of creative autonomy. Entitlement can, for instance, enable one to take risks by investing trust in new relationships.

43

Horizontal Relationships and Entitlement

Relationships always carry tensions between the interests of the parties involved. Two or more people will never have a total confluence of interests. The therapist must understand that even closely related persons will have conflicting interests; in fact, close relationships are more likely to reveal the conflicts. The closer the relationship, the more focus on idiosyncractic needs and convictions. Each person in the relationship has conditions for establishing and maintaining his or her own rights and interests. Consequently, conflicts of interests are inevitable in close-knit relationships, such as families.

> A middle-aged couple—the woman a physiotherapist, the man a physician—have clashing interests. The woman wants to resume her work on a part-time basis after an interruption of several years following the birth of their two children. Her husband is both unwilling and unable to give up his full-time position and, for that matter, cannot take over partial care of the children as his wife would wish.

Conflicts of interests come sharply to the fore in symmetrical (equally obliged) relationships and are the source of larger conflicts. Equity in the balance of give and take can, in symmetrical relationships, be judged only over a long period of time and should never be measured on a moment-to-moment basis. Otherwise there will always be advantages and disadvantages for one person or the other. Momentarily one can feel hurt or exploited by the partner, but in spite of this the relationship as a whole can be viable when the trustworthiness is measured over a long period of time.

If one takes into account the interests of the other, he is entitled to the care and acknowledgment of the other. In symmetrical relationships, the balance of fairness can indeed become unjust if one party's investment exceeds the other's.

Facts of life can change drastically the symmetry of horizontal relationships. For instance, should one of the partners suffer brain damage as the result of an accident, a certain form of asymmetry comes into being. The search for a just balance then becomes an enormous task. Less dramatic events can also upset or disturb the equilibrium of mutual fairness in otherwise symmetrical relationships.

The search for this equilibrium remains a vital task in the ever-changing course of a long-term relationship: maintaining the balance in motion.

Vertical Relationships and Inherent Entitlement

It is apparent that the balance of obligations in asymmetrical relationships cannot be in a simple equilibrium. This is most evident at the beginning and the end of the course of life, namely with the newborn child and the aged parent. Being entitled to care and the giving of care cross each other in the rise and fall of the course of life of child and parent. The asymmetry in parent-child relationships makes its balance of justice fundamentally different from that in horizontal relationships. Constant care is demanded of the parents of small children; the child is entitled to it, for it could not survive without that care. We can speak, therefore, of the inherent entitlement of the small child from whom no return can yet be expected.

The call for trustworthy behavior is nowhere felt so fundamentally as in the care of a helpless, newborn infant. Whether or not the parent enjoys taking care of the newborn, he or she is put to a severe test of accountability. Yet there are parents who cannot respond to the appeal because they themselves have been too deprived in their youth. The child continues to invest trust over a long period of time; herein, occasionally, a positive process within the parents can be set in motion. One might postulate on empirical grounds that the child creates a natural reservoir of trust from which it can later draw.

The observations of Harlow* on maternally deprived mon-
keys, whose disturbance was caused by the isolation in which
they were raised provide a poignant example of this inborn tendency: The little monkey-baby persistently seeks physical contact with the mother, in spite of her tendency to abuse the
little one.

Those parents whose reservoirs of trust have been emptied by
the lack of mutuality with their own parents will not be able to be
a source of nurturance for the firstborn baby. Yet from the per-
sistent trust of the small child a mutuality of caring can be set in
motion. If the mother responds to the trust with increased caring
for the child, the self-reinforcing spiral of earning entitlement
comes into operation, and "mothering" may be more successful
with the second child because the basis for merited trust has
already been established.

> Lydia, an unmarried mother of 17, had an attitude toward
> her baby which offered little hope of her ever caring for her
> son. In the baby's quarter of the residential home where
> mother and child stayed the staff made a great effort to care
> for the baby in such a way that Lydia—as much as was
> possible—experienced only the happy feelings that time
> spent with her child could afford. The staff spared her any
> unpleasant associations, and, gradually, Lydia's visits with
> her child grew longer. Eventually, she was able to comfort
> the infant when he cried—whereas once she could suffer
> him only when he smiled.

While parents can grow through the "giving" trust of even the
newborn child, it is possible for children to be made overly accountable. They serve, sometimes, to provide security for young
parents, who themselves received no support from their parents
or extended families. With the composition of today's nuclear
family—adult generation and one or two children—it is no sim-

---

*Harlow, H.F. in *The Affectional Systems: Behavior of Nonhuman Primates.* Vol. 2.
Edited by A.M. Schrier, H.F. Harlow, F. Stollnitz. New York: Academic
Press, 1965.

ple task to find a balance of give and take that does not place too much responsibility on either side.

Of late the idea has been raised to bring grandparents into the family circle to a greater extent and even to plan the construction of houses (like the "kangaroo houses" of the Netherlands) so that the elderly are no longer expelled from their (extended) families to be isolated in homes for the aged. In our opinion not only the grandparents but also the parents and certainly the grandchildren could benefit from closer contact among the three generations.

Parent-child relationships may be decisively influenced by legacy expectations, but they are also influenced by the asymmetry of power, the unequal power which exists between parents and their dependent children. Parents can never demand full repayment from the child. The child cannot give birth to the parents or repay the fundamental care for survival, though perhaps this can be repaid to aged, sick parents. The combination of the power position of the parents and the devotion and loyalty of the child creates the heavy parental responsibility. A trustworthy relationship between parents and children is the very fiber of existence; it can be reached by providing care without the expectation of symmetrical repayment, drawing on the reward of earned entitlement instead.

Parents may also misuse their power vis-à-vis their vulnerable child and make the child inordinately responsible. We will return to this possibility when we discuss destructive entitlement.

That parents should not "overcharge" their children does not mean that they cannot call on the children for support; it is how children learn to bear responsibility. Moreover, children—even at a very young age—have a need to express caring and affection. One can even say that the child has a right to give of himself or herself.

Many parents do not notice the efforts of their children to please or comfort them. Yet it is of utter importance that they both notice and acknowledge this. Otherwise, they miss out on the very source of warmth for which they so often long. If they

have themselves suffered from lack of trust and acknowledgment, they may believe that they are not entitled.

> A mother and her five-year-old son returned by train from
> the court where her divorce was pronounced. When the boy
> noticed that his mother was crying, he tried to divert her at-
> tention and asked that she help him count all the cows and
> horses in the pastures along the railroad tracks. When the
> attention of his mother faded, he asked several times to go
> to the bathroom. His mother was annoyed. When the son
> was asked in a family therapy session if he helped his
> mother sometimes when she was sad, he gave this example.
> It was evident that the mother had not understood his ef-
> forts to comfort her.

What is at stake here is the *measure* in which care is given and
received: It should correspond with the asymmetry of the
relationship. Sometimes parents behave as if they are the
children because they ask too much care of their children and
give too little in return. In this way *parentification* develops. This
may prove detrimental for the child because the obligations are
too onesided.

As the children mature and the parents age, their relationship
becomes more symmetrical. However, many parents are so accustomed to giving to their children, to filling (loading) their side
of the balance, that they deny their children the chance to fill the
other scale. In other words, they deny their children the right—
and need—to give back. Middle-aged parents may perceive taking from their children as a sign of their lack of independence:
"We still can manage; we don't want to burden our children."
Sometimes children have to wait until parents fall ill or show the
infirmity of old age before they can finally pay back (return the
care) and thus restore the balance. In this way, most wait until the
new asymmetry of the relationships has become clearly visible.

It is important to emphasize here that investment of care and
trust in asymmetrical relationships is always of great significance
for the person who invests. For even if the other is unable or un-

willing to give in return, the earned merit and the connected entitlement remain in force.

> Carla, a 30-year-old woman with many psychosomatic complaints and suffering from sleeplessness, had not visited her senile mother for one year. She had resisted doing so on the advice of her family doctor because he believed that a visit would make her too depressed. When she decided nonetheless to go to her mother and to visit her regularly, this action freed her from her somatic complaints; her serious sleeplessness lessened as well. This all happened in spite of the fact that her mother could not give her any sign of recognizing her.

Cutting off vital relationships—for instance, with the parents —irrevocably entails loss of entitlement. One might suppose that such alienation can provide a solution by way of eliminating the painful confrontations the relationship brings. But this severing of ties is at great cost because one loses opportunities to earn the merit by which one becomes entitled. As a result, in losing earned merits (entitlement), the individual's inner freedom to enjoy life is damaged.

Simple examples from daily life can illustrate this. Much energy can be lost in the vague feeling of being obliged while remaining unable to deal with it concretely and thus continually postponing repayment of the obligation. This is all the more intense and confounding when it concerns care or attention for vital, primary relationships in the family of origin.

The balances of fairness within parent-child and husband/wife relationships are interdependent. The young mother who fulfills her obligation to the infant and then feels tied to the house needs concrete support from her working husband. Without that, her personal needs may become so frustrated that her ability to give to her child suffers. Whereas she earns merit and entitlement in the vertical relationship, she may still become emotionally depleted, placing a demand for adult contact on her husband, who could help her to recuperate and give according to the

child's needs. If the husband cannot see the depleting demands
of his wife's task, he may feel unfairly used, or manipulated. The
heaviness of the task in the vertical relationship creates a relative
asymmetry in the horizontal relationship.

When the scales of giving and receiving become too unbalan-
ced, one partner may decide to break off the relationship and
desert the other. Asymmetrical, vertical relationships, however,
are existentially unbreakable.

If the broken relationship results in divorce, and there are
children involved, it is of most importance that the separating
parents realize that this unbreakable bond between parent and
child *always* remains in force for *both* parents.

Injustice and Destructive Entitlement

In everyone's life unjust events occur; they vary from small to
great injustices. One may suffer the early loss of a father or
mother, or be exposed to the breakup of one's family caused by
divorce, or contract at an early age diabetes or some other
debilitating disease that requires a lifetime of attention.

All of these are facts of life and strike one as unfair when com-
pared to the degrees of injustice which most people have to face.
Existential injustice such as this leads to one form of "destructive
entitlement." Having been wronged when a helpless child earns
one a justification (or entitlement) to compensation although
no one may own up to responsibility for the detrimental effects.
As soon as it is taken out on an innocent person, destructive entitlement becomes the source of new unfairness.

Unfair circumstances in life grant entitlement to the person
who has suffered from the injustice without his being obliged to
give in return. In this respect it is comparable to the inherent entitlement of the newborn, who also is entitled without owing
a return.

This outcome is in clear contrast with the usual course of
events in life in which entitlement parallels earned merit. We
must earn our entitlement—and more so to the extent that we
have been fortunate in life. By contrast, the power of one's

position—for instance, belonging to an influential family—may induce one to claim entitlement without, from an ethical point of view, having personally earned it.

If we have experienced sufficient trust and justice, then we can find ways of coping with the injustices which occur in all of our lives.

Lack of Trust and Destructive Entitlement

The injustice which one must bear in the course of one's life has a heavier weight if that injustice is linked to the lack of trust that one suffered as a child.

The inherent entitlement of the newborn increases when the parents do not take proper care of the infant. Parents who have suffered greatly themselves from injustice sometimes expect unfulfillable trustworthiness from their children. They ask so much that the child must fail and as such becomes for the parents further proof of the ongoing lack of trustworthiness. By demanding that the child be unreasonably responsible and by not acknowledging the child's giving and caring but, on the contrary, blaming him for his failure, parents can burden the child with a never-ending feeling of indebtedness. Although the child becomes overentitled by merited trust, he receives no evidence of it and therefore has no sense of the entitlement.

The child's experience has been that trusting and being trustworthy yield no rewards; he loses trust in the world and develops a desire and right for revenge. But revenge on whom? If the justified claim of revenge is exacted arbitrarily, the revenger creates new injustice. In a destructively entitled person, the self-correcting function of remorse (the experience of guilt over harming someone) is inoperative.

Destructive entitlement has both valid and invalid elements which are at work simultaneously and form an inner contradiction. The valid element has its roots in the past and provides the right to compensation for injury. The invalid element involves the exacting of revenge on innocent parties. Tragically, it is a condition that can burden one for a lifetime. Acting unjustly toward innocent others provides only negative experiences for the agent of the injustice and he misses the opportunity to earn trust and entitlement. Applicable again here is the concept of the *revolving slate* which is presented at the wrong address, often to the partner or the next generation and then in increased measure. People caught in this escalation are unable to benefit others. Their vague feeling of guilt about this inability can be one source of depression.

Some people lead a life in which no single right can be earned: psychotic patients, tucked away in a psychiatric hospital on a long-term basis, or drug addicts whose lives are so much ruled by the dependency on drugs that the interests of others are no longer considered.

A destructive attitude towards others is often coupled with an equally destructive attitude towards oneself. It seems as if one has to burden oneself with perfidy in order to confirm continuously that the world is untrustworthy and that one is being exploited. The blind spot in regard to one's own contribution further confirms the experience of being a victim and produces new evidence of the lack of trustworthiness in the world around oneself.

> A father was raised in the households of several different family members. He did not recognize his parents when he returned home at the age of eight and had never seen his brothers and sister. He remained an outsider and became the scapegoat of the family. This upbringing made him extremely sensitive to injustice. Any perception of injustice in his present environment causes him to become totally enraged. His wife has to protect "her" children against her husband. His family fears the outbursts resulting from this attitude and the father, consequently, has again become an outcast (outsider) within his own nuclear family.

The Significance of Mobilizing Trust and Caring in Contextual Therapy

Does the possibility exist of freeing someone from the vicious circle of destructive entitlement and the connected injustice for oneself and the others?

Lack of acknowledgment of the experienced injustice and of the damaged trust will continually feed the need for destruction.

The therapist should first pay attention to the credit earned by past victimization and then to the sorrow, pain, and anger which accompanied the unjust experiences. Only after the sufferer's unjust fate has been acknowledged and understood can he begin to understand the damaging effect of his own behavior on others. Any sign, however small, of consideration for others— signs often overlooked by the person himself—can provide the catalyst for self-validating growth.

> A divorced mother of 35 cannot care for her three children because of her alcoholism. The children are placed in an institution. She damages her own health and is unable to accept advice or aid. But when she visits the children once a week, she does not drink because she does not want her children to see their mother in such a helpless state.

The chances are that no one notices this exceptional effort. The therapist, who can estimate the real value of this concern, can help the mother to experience earned merit. Temporarily, the therapist is probably the only one who has an eye for the minimal signs of responsible behavior. On the basis of acknowledgment, the taking of responsibility and the giving of care can be reactivated.

Most likely the partner is also damaged by his or her suffering from injustice. Thus, it is improbable that one can give to the other the acknowledgment that he seeks. Consequently, the therapist's ability to discover in every family member earned merit which can lead to acknowledgment is of vital importance. This can be linked with an appeal to one's sense of responsibility. The greatest therapeutic leverage may be provided by invoking the duty of parents to care responsibly for their children. Unused resources of trust between family members and partners in other important relationships can be discovered and activated. Regardless of the original complaint, the goal is always to enable family members to gain trust in each other because of everyone's intrinsic investment in trustworthiness.

It goes without saying that only the therapist, who is convinced that all involved prefer acknowledgment and care to destruction, is able to discover minimal signs of responsibility. His growing conviction that even in the midst of major ruptures great resources are available justifies the tenacity of the Contextual therapist.

4

A FAMILY INTERVIEW WITH IVAN BOSZORMENYI-NAGY

For many years Nagy has travelled regularly to Europe, lecturing on Contextual Therapy. He connects his theoretical lectures with actual practice by interviewing families referred to him for consultation. The format is that of a workshop or seminar with a number of therapists among whom are those who have been working with the families.

The families are informed that a group of family therapists is observing their sessions with Nagy. The therapists observe the proceedings from an adjoining room via a one-way mirror. The post-session discussion between Nagy and the group of observing therapists provides ample opportunity to understand more clearly the theoretical starting points of the Contextual approach.

The following is an interview which Nagy conducted some years ago, given to us by the therapist who was treating this family. It deals with a problem between generations that is so common it will seem to many as if their own problems are reflected. It is also an illustration of the dilemma often experienced by the therapist, who starts on Nagy's road but encounters difficulties in developing sufficient expressiveness to motivate the family members to undertake the rejunctive steps.

In spite of the fact that during this interview only the spouses are present, it will be clear that we are dealing here with a "family interview" in which all members are involved. It is a family with three children, ages eight, six and four. The couple have been married for 10 years. The couple requested therapy because of marital problems. The wife, especially, is depressed and dissatisfied with her marital life. Both partners have been involved in extramarital relationships. According to the wife, they cannot settle an argument because he withdraws rather than fight for his point of view. As a result, it is the wife who must constantly make allowances and reconcile differences at the end of the argument.

The couple states repeatedly that they have no problems with their children: They are kind to the children, they are good parents, and the children themselves have no problems. The therapy has been going on for two or three months. The husband had been reluctant to participate, but nonetheless he did most of the time.

This particular family was selected for the workshop because of the wife's tendency to connect "spontaneously" her marital problems with thoughts about her mother. According to the wife, Mrs. A, she is not liked by her mother. She claims: "I am too much like my father. I resemble him. I have his character. I am an introvert. I am a secretive person." She would like to improve her relationship with her mother, but she is not optimistic about the chances for success. Her father died before she married. Her mother remarried. She can get along better with her mother-in-law than with her own mother.

The husband, Mr. A, has a difficult family background. He has two sisters. Both his parents are still alive. Discussions with him have revealed that his relationship with his father is extremely troubled. For six years they have had virtually no close contact, although his father lives in the same town.

Mr. A's father is described as a cruel man, hard and hot-tempered, who used to brutally beat his young son. He was raised in a strict Protestant household by parents who felt bound by their religion to have many children. He had a difficult childhood and bears a continuing resentment because, following his own father's death, his mother and older brother grew closer and opportunities forbidden to him were permitted to his brother. The grandfather, Mr. A's father, is said to have beaten his wife frequently.

Recently, Mr. A was shocked by his own actions; in a fury, he had beaten one of his children. He started to cry, blamed himself, and reminisced about his having been battered by his own father.

When the therapist suggested to the husband that he should work to improve his relationship with his father—since avoiding the father, who is also grandfather to the Mr. and Mrs. A's two children, amounts to a stagnant family relationship—he stated that he had no interest in doing so. He did not even actively hate his father. In the son's eyes, his father was beneath contempt. At the insistence of the therapist, however, the husband presented his father with a gift, a book on a subject which interested him. The father received it kindly, and with sincere thanks.

The husband's mother also came from a strict, duty-oriented family. She wanted to achieve some education and pursue a career as a nurse, but instead, out of duty, she devoted herself to motherhood. More recently, as his mother suffered from problems with her heart and was told by her doctor that there must be a psychosomatic component in the illness resulting from the tension between her husband and herself, Mr. A went to his sisters in an attempt to discuss with them the possibility of improving their parents' marriage. The sisters apparently discouraged these efforts, claiming that their father was just a selfish, childish man who was not about to change.

Commentary by Nagy on the Basis of the Previous Data

It is important to note here that this is exactly the point at which both society and most therapists are inclined to give up on the allegedly bad relations. By contrast, in the Contextual approach, with its principle of rejunction through therapy, such a stagnation is never accepted without a serious attempt to develop some of the trustworthiness resources in a seemingly non-trustworthy, depleted, parent-child relationship. Since both husband and wife reveal that they are still engaged in extramarital affairs, the Contextual therapist has to consider at this point the existence of a covertly mutual and collusive behavior pattern in which husband and wife try to remedy their resentment, contempt, and other negative feelings toward their families of origin through scapegoating the marriage. In this case, the affairs can serve as evidence of disloyalty and lack of commitment to the marriage, with the connotation of invisible loyalties to the parents of the respective families of origin.

At this point one begins to wonder how much to trust the parents' claim that the children are unaffected and free of problems. It is easy to perceive the situation as an example of parents borrowing from the resources of the future. Naturally, also involved in this collusively exploitative "borrowing" is the parents' immunity to any guilt that might have resulted from their harming the children. Dynamically, that immunity originates from the so-called "revolving slate," according to which an unadmitted invisible loyalty to one's parent can overfulfill one's obligation of filial legacy and thereby make one insensitive to the guilt of failing to satisfy the legacy of parenthood. Such insensitivity to remorse can be a sign, also, of a person's earned destructive entitlement.

As a general rule in such cases, the therapist should refrain from asking the children to report on their parents in what might be considered disloyal fashion. However, credit and acknowledgment should be extended to the children in recognition of the difficulty of their situation. The therapist should expect that the parents, too, acknowledge their children's concern and care for their struggling parents.

The contrast between the wife's good relationship with her in-laws and her bad relationship with her own mother creates an intrinsically treacherous loyalty situation. In this regard, she could endorse her husband's seeking to retrieve his loyalty toward his father, thereby consolidating the marriage. On the other hand, she could burden her own marital commitment with the disloyalty of preferring her in-laws to her own parent.

A Family Interview

Following is the text of the interview which Nagy conducted with the couple; Nagy added later the annotations printed in the right-hand column.

The interview begins. Present are: Nagy, husband, wife, and the original therapist.

IBN: I have heard a little about you and your families. I have a number of thoughts, and I understand you must have some questions. But in my mind, the children figure very strongly. As you perhaps know, I see many families, and I am always very concerned about the children. I am not comfortable about leaving them out. But that is a general thought; I don't know what to do about that at this point.

I indicate my concern about the children, even though I have never met them. By the principle of multilateral balances of fairness, I feel at least as strongly committed to the children as to the adults. I wonder how it could be possible that in such a disturbed marriage the children are just fine. On the other hand, before I know more about specifics, it would be strategically unwise to argue for what amounts to an explicit accusation of the couple as inconsiderate parents. The danger of siding with the children's interests is negligible because all parents have vital investments in the welfare and survival interests of their children. By standing firm on my demand for responsible parenting, I increase the depth of the ethical base of my contract with the parents, too.

Hus: Our children, or the children of her mother and father and of my mother and father?

The father seems concerned with conveying to me that their therapist has worked with the intergenerational model, attributed to my writings.

IBN: Well, all of them, of course, are of concern to me. Now I am even thinking of

I inject the notion of the temporal perspective of concern about the children's de-

your children's children, who are certainly not here yet. But I am more concerned with how we can improve the future than with how we can change the past. What are the most important questions? Did you both write up questions or just you? Select the most important one, please.

velopmental vulnerability, concern about future generations, and the high priority I give to benefits that reach into the formative dynamics of future children and grandchildren.

Hus: The most important question is that because of the therapy I have to talk to my father, and that is very difficult because he doesn't want to talk about things which have to do with his feelings and emotions. He tries to evade those feelings. When I ask him about his youth, he doesn't want to talk about it. He can talk about his work, very generally. If you ask him a personal question, he evades it or he stands up and walks away. I don't know how I can talk to him. This is a main point.

The father openly presents himself as a dependent "patient" who follows therapeutic prescriptions without strong self-motivation or conviction.

The father sounds as if he is giving a professional description of his futile efforts at making his father express his emotions—as if expression of feelings and "changing" the paternal grandfather were significant therapeutic goals. Furthermore, since this is a training interview, I begin to wonder: Is the intergenerational approach being used by the therapist only in a psychological (multiple individual) context? Is there room for developing its most significant, ethical contextual leverage?

IBN: Why would you make the effort? For whose benefit?

I challenge the father to take a stand on what he is willing to work on in this session.

Hus: For myself. To have better relations between him and myself.

He sounds compliant.

IBN: Do you think it would help you?

Attempt to make the father accountable for his stated position.

Hus: I doubt it, but I am told experiences in this kind of work have proved that it can be good if you go to the roots of the problem in one's own family.

Sounds like a mocking comment on my role as the teacher of the couple's therapist.

IBN: How much do you think you owe your parents as a child? Or do you think you have overpaid your debts, so to speak, as a child?

I attempt to cut through this fencing match that is developing and expect explorations on a deeper, ethical balance level. I make a sudden transition from behavioral descriptions of the father's futile efforts at reaching his allegedly inhuman father to a question pertaining to the balance of merits and fairness in the father-grandfather relationship. The quick transition to the ethical context serves to accelerate the teaching benefit of the session.

Hus: I am afraid I don't understand the question.

He needs time for answering this.

IBN: It was a difficult question. Considering what a child owes to his parents— have you paid back more than you have received? More than what you could be expected to repay? I thought that you might have some feelings about this.

Hus: I don't know how much a child is indebted to his parents. What kinds of debt has to be paid?

IBN: I am not talking about a child. I am asking you. You don't have to have an answer to that. My point is that if you are made to improve your relationship with your father without any conviction, then you should work on this question. Naturally, if you see no sense in this question, you might direct your attention elsewhere. I understand that your mother is sick and that your father has had a heart attack.

Hus: I don't know what kind of sickness he had. He couldn't speak, he had trouble breathing.

IBN: Well, let's not get into the medical part of it. Let's try it the other way around.

I make room for a delayed answer (moratorium) and also allow for a possible refusal of the answer.

To make the father accountable for a meaningful subjective goal of all this therapeutic effort.

To concretize the same issue: Do the parents need attention in their current health problem?

I explore assets of trustworthiness in the family. Also, it is time now that the

What is good now in the family? *(turns to wife)* I hear that you have a good relationship with your mother-in-law. Is that correct? So that is at least one positive thing.

Theoretically, it could help your marriage. You know, many young women have a negative relationship with their mother-in-law.

therapist involve the wife in the conversation. In certain European families this might be important to remember because of the wife's traditionally subservient role: She defers to her husband, leaves to him the interaction with strangers.

I probe into the trustworthiness resource of a woman-to-woman relationship.

Wife: I know.

IBN: I could speculate that your positive attitude may connect the two families in some degree. Maybe that helps you also with your own parents. How do you answer my question: What is really good in the family, something that one can build on? So far we seem to be charging a brick wall. Is it a dead-end road to try to make your husband talk to his father when it is so difficult? His father doesn't want to talk and his sisters tell him not to bother, that he is not worth the effort. Where is something that we can build on? Where is some strength or something good in this family?

Resource orientation applied instead of futile attacks on pathology.

Are trust resources of husband's family too restricted?

Wife: The good thing is that everyone in his family has a good relationship with his mother. The problem is that his mother has been discharged from the hospital and we are afraid that she will have a heart attack again. And the problem is what to choose: Either to say to his mother not to go back home both for her own sake and for ours because we care about her? Or to let her go back knowing that she may have another heart attack? When we suggest to her not to go back, it hurts his father.

Wife points out the source of trustworthiness in paternal grandmother's relationships. She voices a need for protecting her from her husband, the grandfather, who it is alleged, is capable of killing his wife.

She describes the components of her husband's split filial loyalty.

IBN: You mean she would live with you? Has she ever stayed with you in the past?

I register surprise in order to emphasize the importance of the underlying split loyalty issue.

Wife: Yes, she stayed with us for a while. She is a very easy person to live with.

Hus: The question is how to protect my mother from getting another heart attack.

IBN: There is a question in my mind at this point. When you said that there is a resource in the good relationship that everyone may be having with his mother, it sounded encouraging. Per-

I question whether the split loyalty situation may under mine the resource charac-

haps we can utilize that resource for further im-
provements. But then, if
grandmother's goodness
leads to the need for protecting her from the badness of
grandfather, I begin to
worry. That sounds like husband has to have a split
loyalty to his two parents
and—in all my experience—
that is horrible. Because then
he has to be in the middle,
and even your children are
in the middle. They have to
be the judges and say:
"Grandfather is no good because he destroys
grandmother—and she has
to be saved from him."

I don't see how anyone
can win at this point. It is a
losing position to be in. So
what are some other ways?
That's the question. And I
hear your sisters say that the
relationship with the grandfather cannot be changed,
that it is a hopeless and bad
relationship. Everybody has
done as much as possible
and nothing has worked.
And where does that leave
everybody? What does it
mean?

Hus: We think it would be

teristic of a good relationship
with the paternal
grandmother.

The split loyalty is a severely
detrimental condition.

I search for resource utilization rather than reiteration of
pathology.

Back to a pathology orienta-

very difficult to change a person who is almost 70.

IBN: That's the second question. The first question is this: Can you yourself benefit from making the effort? Because we are hung up too much on this. But it is a big problem. It may be the most difficult problem only because it is so much in our awareness.

Now, as to the second question. If I understand you, you and your two sisters take the position that why should he change at 70 if he has not been able to change until now? And you do nothing but write him off as someone who is no good, hopeless, inhuman. Apparently, he is a "monster." But who knows how many years your father has remaining? Some day he will die, and my question is: What is best for you and your two sisters and even for your children and grandchildren? Even if your father cannot change but the three of you together

tion. The futility of the individual-oriented thinking is clearly showing here. The task is impossible: to change another person against his will.

Frontal attack on pathology orientation. Also, at this point another important therapeutic "technical" principle emerges: the management of dependent passitivity through the expectation of an accountable attitude. The assumption that their aged father has to change can contain a dependent longing on the part of grown-up children. As in the case of this husband and his sisters, the issue comprises both realistic and ethical justice considerations. The adult offspring have to be made accountable for their position if any active strategy is to be pursued.

The issue of health brought in as a resource.

Long-term questions of satisfaction . . . legacy of parental accountability utilized as motivators. Can they move

are trying to help—notice I did not say change. Would that not make you feel better than knowing that you had written him off before he died and you had done nothing? What would be better for your children and grandchildren?

See, I am just separating the question of what makes you, your sisters, and your children feel better from this matter of whether or not your father changes visibly, observably. I don't know what change is, change can be anything—something that you can see or something that is in the heart, I don't know. But I want to ask again whether you want to leave yourself and your sisters and their children and your children and their children with the thought that you have given up or would you in the end feel better knowing that you have tried, regardless of what the old man's responses seem to be? (*to wife*) Now, with you, however, I am wondering how can you balance your relationship with your own family and with your hus-

the family out of the stagnant overt hatred and contempt of the paternal grandfather? Can the husband's attempts to help his father provide satisfaction without manifest results: the grandfather's changed behavior?

I reinforce the legacy pressure.

This is the therapeutic plan in a nutshell: The ethical rebalancing has to be in the original relational context, but it does not depend on visible actions; it relies on serious intention and on trial action.

In actual therapy another major exploration would pertain to the circumstance that the wife may injure her loyal-

band and his family? Seemingly, you have a better relationship with his mother than with your own mother. Is that correct? What does that do to you and your relationships? Have you discussed that with the therapist? Do you have any thoughts about it?

Wife: I thought we didn't talk at all.

Therapist: Do you mean what her relationship with her mother-in-law does to her relationship with her own mother? No, I have left that out. I did not realize that that could be important.

IBN: Well, it is easy for me to ask questions, being a visitor. I am going back to America, and he is your therapist, and I am just talking about what comes to my mind. If I were you and I were to say, "Here is a woman who is more of a mother to me than my own mother," then I would start feeling disloyal to my own mother. I might rub it in: "Look, I have a better relationship with that other woman." Am I in a kind of a

ty to her mother by placing her mother-in-law higher. Unless she gives attention to the disloyalty aspect of this preference, her marital attitude may suffer (revolving slate).

By taking distance from the therapist role, I actually reinforce my impact, even though it is delivered in a condensed, short-term format.

war and is this the heaviest ammunition I can shoot at my mother? Do I hope that my mother will see this, and then she will change her mind and be kinder to me? Will she be jealous that I have a better relationship with someone else? I have seen this happen in various families.

Does the wife use her preference for mother-in-law as an overt weapon against her own mother?

Wife: I have a good relationship with his mother, but I am fonder of my mother. When I really have to choose, I choose my own mother.

IBN: But then what can you do for your own mother?

Wife: I have seven brothers and sisters, and I always had other mothers around me in my life: mothers of my friends and my mother's sister, who was like a mother to me, too. Because my mother was always busy and I was one of seven children, some of my brothers and sisters had more of her attention because of their natures, I think.

The wife describes a long-term pattern of substitution as a weapon in a war of retaliation against her mother's alleged favoritism vis-á-vis her children.

IBN: How is it the other way around? Can you give to your mother? Does she re-

Another major therapeutic principle of the Contextual approach is the utilization of

ceive willingly if you want to give her something? Can you think of an example?

the dependent member's hidden capacity for account-ability as a major resource. At the same time the question is examined: Is her mother a non-receptive parent?

Wife: Yes, I can. I tried many times, I think, and many times she didn't accept what I had to offer. She didn't understand what I was trying to do.

Her mother is essentially the non-receiving type, a parent one has to remain totally accountable to.

IBN: Do you remember a time when she *did* accept what you tried to give? I don't necessarily mean material things—it may have been attention or kindness.

In therapy it would be important to find out ways and means by which the maternal grandmother is able and willing to accept giving on her daughter's part, in essence, through offering concern. This investigation already counts as an input into ethical rebalancing.

Wife: Yes, I can remember.

IBN: What, for instance?

Wife: That was before my father died, I think.

IBN: Has it changed since then?

Wife: I think so.

IBN: Is it more difficult for her to accept from you? Can she accept from your brothers more easily?

Wife: From some of my brothers and sisters, yes, better.

Does this selective non-receptiveness signify a hidden parentification of the wife by her mother? Does the maternal grandmother have an inclination to hold on to this daughter through infinite, unrepayable indebtedness?

IBN: How old is your mother now?

Wife: Sixty-three or sixty-four.

IBN: What comes to my mind is that you may want to have a better relationship with her and yet she doesn't accept things from you. And she is not in any need. She is not sick. She is, in fact, well. I understand, she has a friendship—

The interviewer offers an avenue for the investigation of potential realistic needs the grandmother may have: Is her health condition affected by aging?

Wife: No, she is married.

IBN: A marriage which seems to be a satisfactory relationship. So, how can you give to her now? Well, again the children come to my mind. Do you have any thought of how the children come into this now?

Ordinarily, the grandmother-grandchild relationship presents a great resource for trust and giving.

Wife: Our own children?

IBN: Her grandchildren. Does she have many grandchildren?

Wife: Fifteen.

IBN: What about your mother and your children?

Wife: It's the same, not any different. It is not the same as with his mother. Because my mother has so many, I think.

Wife sounds as if she is protecting her mother and children as well.

IBN: Well, I can understand what you are saying: If she has many grandchildren, she cannot give as much attention to all of them as she could to one or two. But are you saying something else, that she really treats your children as if they were not close to her or not as good as her other grandchildren?

Wife: No, that's not what I mean. I just think that she is not a motherly type. She doesn't have the children with her much, but she didn't spend much time with her own children either. She said once that she is not a real mother.

Wife exonerates her mother's attitude by a psychological characterization: The grandmother labels herself as "not a real mother."

IBN: That is important if she gives excuses and regrets that she could not do better.

Is this an area where the grandmother could be helped with her own indebtedness out of failure of parenting?

Wife: I think she is feeling guilty about her not giving enough affection to her own children.

IBN: But on the other hand she gave physical life to so many children. That is an interesting thing. Because if it's not affection, it's still something. I mean, she certainly is a parent. She gave that many lives, at least physically. She has paid her obligation. Do you have a comment on that question originally asked of your husband? Whether you have overpaid or underpaid as a child?

Interviewer begins to explore the ethical balance of the parent-child context. A mother's entitlement does not chiefly depend on her behavioral attitudes but on the legacy of the fact of having been a parent. In the case of a mother, this means, of course, the physical giving of life.

Wife: I don't think anyone has to *pay* anything. I think that is the wrong word.

The language of hard accountability in parent-child relationships is offensive, even though meaningful at the same time.

IBN: What word would you like to use?

Wife: No one asked to come into this world. To be born.

Wife may be defending herself against the overt, traditional expectations of filial indebtedness.

IBN: Well, that's true. But if no one takes care of me, I may be born, but I am not going to survive. So someone takes care of me, gives me food and shelter. Otherwise I

I attempt to present the impersonal factual truth of the legacy of existential indebtedness for life and survival as a human universal.

wouldn't survive. But I realize I am asking the wrong
question. Neither of you likes
my question. I feel sort of
like Moses presenting the
Fifth Commandment
"Honor thy father and thy
mother". It does not say
whether you asked to be
born or not. That would require a rewritten Fifth
Commandment: *"Providing
you asked to be born, honor thy
father and thy mother."*

Allusion to the divine Commandment is another, cultur-
ally widespread way of separating the legacy of filial
loyalty, from the merit of the
parent's manifest behavior
toward the child, e.g., being
a "bad mother."

Wife: Perhaps we don't like
the question because both of
our parents, his and mine,
told us when we were young:
"We get this and that, and
that, and that, and that, and
that for you and now you are
an ungrateful child. You do
this to us?" We have heard it
too often, and that's why we
do not like the word "pay."

Overtly accountable to the
parents. The interviewer may
sound like a (realistic and
transference) replica of the
parents of the spouse.

This is a change of attitude:
the wife is willing to respond
to the framework of filial
obligation and explains the
reason for her and her husband's previous reluctance
for same.

IBN: O.K., so they talked
about the obligation to repay, that makes sense. I remember a mother who once
said, "My child was to me
like a bank account, and now
I expect it to repay my investment." So you, too, were

made to feel that you have an obligation to repay. That may not be such a bad thing.

I think it is true that children are indebted to repay something, not only to their parents but also to their children when they have children. Yet if you are always told you owe this much and yet you are not allowed to repay anything at all, then I can imagine that my question must have annoyed you.

Overt ways of making children accountable for receiving from their parents are more customary in traditional societies than in the U.S. These blunt allegations are easier to handle; in fact, the blunter they are, the more so.

Wife: My husband was told by his father: "You owe me so much." And there were so many times his father wronged him. I can imagine he doesn't like this.

The wife refers again to the paternal grandfather's alleged harsh oppressiveness which, she implies should cancel out his claim to deserving his son's filial loyalty. Probably, the husband's situation is made even harder because of his family's habit of ascribing the "monster" role to his father. This socially validated scapegoating of his father places on the husband a subtle guilt of being unfair toward his parent. Even if the grandfather's behavior is "objectively" objectionable, this circumstance should not cancel out his legacy-bound merit as a parent. (On a psychological scale, this guilt may be paralleled by the husband's Oedipal victory over his father.)

IBN: Now again your children come to my mind. You would be inclined to place all problems in terms of your father-in-law. Yet this pattern runs from generation to generation. If parents are bitter and they feel their own parents don't deserve gratitude, but they make their own children feel obligated, what will happen then to the next generation? I feel that a balancing happens between the generations. Now again I don't know you well enough, but if I were to work with you, I would work very hard on that balancing.

Suppose you try to break the pattern and try not to do the same as was done to you, and say: "I am not going to make my child accountable." You would have to be superhuman not to wish upon your children what your parents had done to you. You have to absorb the cost of bitterness and hold it within yourself. What will it do to you? Is it even possible to hold it back? Or does it have to spill over to the next generation?

Wife: About my own children —I don't know how much I

I probe a major Contextual therapeutic strategic leverage: 3-generational balancing. As I offer empathic partiality for the spouses in their claims for merit and entitlement as parents, I aim at the next stage of my multidirectional partiality: empathizing with the grandparents in their own roles as parents first and later as children themselves. The complex leverages of interlocking entitlements and debts create a more balanced human context.

I begin to extend multidirected partiality to the spouses as parents and also to their children. Is there a danger that they will inadvertently impose even heavier unrepayable expectations on their children?

While I place heavy accountability for fair parental expectation on the spouses, I offer them as mitigating circumstances the alleged unfairness of the expectations placed upon them by their own parents.

am doing the same. I don't know, I can't see that.

IBN: I must say that if it is only done with words, it's not the worst. You know that is hard enough to deal with. But I have seen that it can be worse if parents say: "You don't owe me anything." Then the child owes everything. Both of you are trapped in a position of warfare or revenge towards your parents. Do you understand what I've said?

I caution the parents about the dangers of a reverse attitude which disclaims all filial indebtedness, leaving the child with an unrequitable existential guilt.

I indicate that the context of a power confrontation vis-á-vis their parents is confusing and possibly detrimental to their chances for reaching a balanced ledger of filial indebtedness.

Therapist: Isn't that true?

Wife: No.

Therapist: Aren't you in a warfare?

The therapist seems to be committed to the transactional context of a "warfare" between the spouses and their respective "bad" parents.

Wife: No, and we both want a change. But we don't see how.

Therapist: Where should the depression come from?

Wife: From feeling not wanted I think.

Therapist: Yes.

IBN: Yes, that is one aspect. Another aspect is when you say: "Since my father died, my mother wouldn't receive from me." And when you were angry at me, when I asked you how much you owed to your parents, your answer was that you don't owe anything, you only were told to think that you do. You are caught between being indebted and your mother's non-receptiveness. How can you win? The only way for you to win is to say: "All this craziness has affected generations and I am going to reverse this now, for myself and for my children."

If you are passive, your children will just sink into the same thing. I am not trying to scare you, and I am not your therapist. But that is my experience with many families. You cannot change your parents—but you can change your own attitude to search for a new pattern of give-and-take with your mother.

Perhaps even your children could do something for her, and it would be easier to make her recognize it. It would simply be more hu-

I offer to untangle the confusion between the ethical and transactional-communicational dimensions of the parent-child context of relationship.

Wife cannot repay because of her mother's non-receptiveness. She is also resentfully rebellious against her parents' overt demands for repayment. The overt value of contemporary social custom stresses the offspring's freedom from all forms of control or rights alleged by the "old-fashioned" parent generation. Yet the bind lies in the offspring's inability to repay on his or her own terms.

An active attitude has to be designed for the benefit of both the spouses and their children.

The goal of changing the spouses' parents' behavior is deceptive and futile.

The grandchildren could be involved in an active rebal-

man. Your mother is 63, she may have many years yet to live. You have to decide whether you can work on a more meaningful relationship with your mother.

It is easy for me to talk about your problem. I have only one brother. My parents are dead, and I don't know what it is like to be one of 11 children. But I would like to tell you something about my own family experience. I always felt that my brother was closer to my mother than I was. I recall an occasion when I was trying to give her something by telling her about something that I had achieved. I thought this would make her happy. Instead, she just turned away and looked at a book. At the time she was almost 80 and visiting as my guest in America. I had the option just to leave it at that. After all, she is old, why bother her, why hurt her while she is my guest? Or I could try to make her accountable for a

ancing strategy for everyone's benefit, including their own. The benefit of successful repayment of existential indebtedness will come from the concerned, responsible efforts themselves. Nonetheless, there should be attempts made to help the grandparents to acknowledge the benefits offered to them.

Having used the couple for a teaching purpose, I offer to give them a personal account of my own relationship. At the minimum, this should equalize the degree of public expense of breaking the couple's privacy of relationships.

I describe moments of my own mother's non-receptiveness.

Which leads to greater trust building: making an aged mother accountable for her nonreceptiveness and non-

fair give-and-take between us.

I decided to try. I said, "Well, I told you something and you didn't give me any response. Yet I think what I said must mean something to you. It means something to me." My mother started to cry and said that her main shortcoming as a mother is that she cannot be affectionate: "Believe me, your success means very much to me, but I couldn't tell you." And she cried, yet I felt the two of us were much more meaningfully related afterwards.

She died about a year or two later. This episode still makes me feel better about my relationship with my mother, and I think it did improve it. My choice to shake her up and confront her improved our relationship. By both giving her something and not letting her be the nonreceptive parent, essentially I told her: "Listen you are the parent and I am your child. We have a human relationship and that's better for both you and me. Let's not turn away from it."

giving attitudes or permitting her to remain shielded off by a marginal relatedness to her son?

I am not telling you to do something just because it was beneficial in my situation. But I, like you, had several options to choose from. I could have sat back and felt sorry for myself, wondering why my mother was not more affectionate and more interested in me. Or I could condemn her and do nothing. Or, finally, I could design a way for both of us to relate as human beings. If I were your therapist, I would help you find some means of relating to your mother.

Contrast between active reaching out in an ethically valid way and a passive hope that the parent will change before dying.

Wife: I have tried already. But it is not easy when you haven't had any contact for years. You have to move very slowly. When I haven't spoken to her for a year, I can't say just as I come into the house, "Here I am! What can I do for you?"

Wife responds in honest detail and concreteness. She points out some of her difficulties in trying exactly the same thing.

IBN: Well, once you know how to try, what can happen? Would you get hurt or would she get hurt?

I explore the concrete circumstances that could expect to evolve if the wife takes a more active stance of trying to break her stagnant relationship with her mother.

Wife: Both.

IBN: Yes, first you should be

prepared to face whether you are still the little girl who is easily hurt by not getting a good response. I can almost predict that you will be hurt. Because chances are that older people do not change that easily. So I could not guarantee that she will change to a more receptive parent. We would have to work on trying to make you stronger so that you can weather a little beating and try it again for your own benefit.

In the process you would have to become the parent and she the baby if she does not know how to be a grown-up partner. In a way you will teach that pattern of responsibility. You would have to be stronger than just a little girl who wants attention. You are now a mother, fighting also for the next generation. You are not just asking a favor for yourself.

At this point I miss your children again. They may even give us a suggestion about what to do. They may understand something important about you and they may be interested in hearing about the business of who

How can the wife's dependent cravings be separated from the criteria of success? It is predictable that she would be hurt through her mother's possibly non-giving attitudes.

The wife must learn to rely upon taking her own accountable step, rather than depend on the prospect of her mother's "change." She will get the reward of the knowledge that her initiative will probably benefit her children as well. They will obtain a firmer base of relational trustworthiness and, therefore, of basic trust for their own psychosocial development.

I tell the parents, the therapist, and the trainee group about a renewed reason for including the children in the therapeutic effort. This will lead to the main recommendation: Would the parents come for a second try and

owes to whom. Your son is only eight, I understand, but even small children understand something like that. So where do we go from here? I have done most of the talking. Do you have any comment at this point?

Hus: You say you want to compare this situation in our family with our fathers and mothers and my wife and I as children years ago. I wonder, is that the same thing? I think I am different from my father and from my mother, and my children are different from what I am, the way I think and what I feel. How could we create a link between my family of the past and my family now?

IBN: I am different from my parents, too. But I come from my parents, that I cannot change.

Hus: Yes, that is true.

IBN: That is what I am talking about.

Hus: Biological link.

IBN: If it were only biological, it would be easier. But I am not here to argue. If you

bring their children to another interview?

The husband states many reasons to resist the basic notion of intergenerational accountability and of transgenerational linkages.

The factual and ethical aspects of the legacy of filial loyalty remain.

don't agree with anything, I
would be the first to say:
Don't do it. I want to find
something that makes sense.
I mean if all of this makes no
sense, then don't do anything
about it. But, then you tell
me, what do you want to do?
I just don't want you to be
passive and sort of throw it
in your therapist's lap. I have
offered something; if it is not
good, what is a workable alternative? You have to take
responsibility for your life
and your family.

I offer to listen to counter-
proposals for therapeutic
strategy, but expect accountable suggestions in return.

Hus: You imply that my children will have the same difficulties as we do because we
had the same situation with
our parents. If that is true, it
means the problem will be
passed on to future generations, and that frightens me.

Husband questions the therapeutic rationale on the basis
of his fears. He is concerned
about the children's future.

IBN: What are your fears?
What could happen to your
children?

Hus: What could happen? I
don't know. Something in
the future.

IBN: Let me ask another
question: Will your children
see their parents split to the
same degree as you and your

The chances of split filial
loyalty are injected as the
children's price to be paid
for noninclusion in the ther-

sisters see your parents being split?

Hus: I hope not.

IBN: Do you think your children see the two of you as closer to each other than you and your sisters saw your parents?

Hus: Yes.

IBN: (*to wife*) What do you think?

Wife: I didn't see my parents as being split.

IBN: How about comparing your children's view of the two of you to the view that your husband and his sisters have of their parents?

Wife: I can't see what kind of influence it has on my children.

IBN: Are you saying that your marriage is as good as it can be?

Wife: We are trying.

Hus: The answer is no.

apeutic plans. The initial problems of marital conflict, threat of divorce, and mutual deceptiveness may present the children with an expectation of split filial loyalty.

Blanket denial of the prospects of split loyalty expectations on her children.

Husband's integrity cannot tolerate the intrinsic irresponsibility of not caring for the children.

IBN: I assume that at a similar age his parents were also saying: "We are trying." When they were your age, I am sure they said they were trying and I am sure that they *were* trying. It is almost impossible that they were not.

Here is my chance to be partial to the grandparents.

Wife: I think only his mother was trying.

The wife resists the inclusion of paternal grandfather into a multidirectional partiality.

Hus: Yes, I would be surprised if my father . . .

The husband follows.

IBN: Yes, I forgot that he is a monster. He is not a human being. He had no feelings whatsoever. I have not seen that yet, but perhaps in this family someone is just a monster. As you talk about trying, your children come to my mind. Your husband admitted honestly that yours is not such a good marriage. You claim that you are trying. The children I am sure are trying even harder than the two of you. Children always try to bring the family together, until they become wholly discouraged. Here I miss your children again. Do you still object to bringing

I use a severe confrontation approach because this may be one of the most crucial points in the session, once the husband admitted the possibility of their marriage not being much better than the one of his parents.

In a new turn, I share with the parents my conviction about the children's actively caring and helpful attitudes toward their family.

your children? (*The parents decline to commit themselves to the suggestion.*) (*to the wife*) Do you cry when you are depressed?

I offer to be partial to mother who appears to be on the verge of tears.

Wife: Sometimes, not very often.

Wife accepts offer of concern.

IBN: Somehow I also feel that you were protecting your mother from me.

I offer a suggestion prompted by the wife's reluctance to deal with her relationship with her mother and her unwillingness to take an active stand against family stagnation.

Wife: Yes, why shouldn't I?

The wife's openness and free expression of resentment is a good response.

IBN: I think you should. You are a loyal daughter. But that is also a great burden for a child—always to make allowances and excuses for the parent.

    You extend advance payments again and again, as most children do. I think you are an overpaying, dutiful daughter who is angry because she has paid so much. But you remain dutiful and loyal to your mother, even in regard to my trying to offer help to the whole family. And probably your children

I acknowledge the value of filial loyalty on the wife's part. At the same time, I diminish the disloyalty implications of her evolving positive transference, intrinsic in her speaking for the good of the whole family.

This is an honest acknowledgment of the overgiving, parentified position in which the mother was cast by her family. This renewed partiality is probably beneficial for building a therapeutic alliance with her while she is

are overly devoted to you. If
you have no other comment
before we stop, my advice is
to work on these points.
Goodbye.

still struggling with her reluctance to heed her parents'
suffering.

5

APPLICATION IN PRACTICE

Since Nagy's concepts derive from empirical clinical work, it is mandatory to learn his concepts through their application to practice and self-experience.

Personal Impact of the Concepts

Throughout our many years as teachers of Contextual Therapy, we have never failed to be struck by the impact Nagy's theories have on each new group of students. Influenced by their recognition of key terms and the intrinsic values attached to them, the students invariably respond with vigor and often powerful emotion. Many react with petulance and resistance as new ethical associations clash with the values of their dogmatic religious upbringings. Almost all are shocked by the intensity of their own responses.

One of the most essential and intrusive vehicles for understanding the ethical nature of human relationships is the exploration during the training period of one's own family of origin. The student is asked to search into previous generations on both sides of his or her family as far back as the great-grandparents if possible. We mean to evoke a sense of heritage by asking questions which provoke a historical perspective of the family of origin, questions directed to the circumstances in which the ancestors lived: What were their social conditions? What were their hopes and expectations, their norms and values, their social perspectives? What was the position of man and woman in the ancestry? The compiled material can be most powerfully revived by including photographs, mementos, and other personal items pertinent to the family history.

We do not prescribe a standard form for presenting the life story; we do not want to suggest that everyone's unique history can be captured schematically. Putting the family tree on paper can be helpful, provided that it does not lead to petrified charts of pathology throughout the generations. The emphasis is on exploring resources of trust. The line of action is to locate the important persons in one's life who are connected with essential events and who can, perhaps, shed light on matters the student wants elucidated—and to reach them without pointing an accusatory finger.

The journey into the past is in itself more important than the amount of information one may gather from that journey. While listening to the family chronicles, we are often struck by how significant a role it played by the religion of the ancestry and the family's struggle for survival and success. In choosing their professions, our students often enter a world in which the values, norms, and ways of life are remote from those of the parental environment.

Viewing their parents in relation to their grandparents' backgrounds can provide some surprising discoveries which may lead to new points of contact between the generations. Students frequently tell of the pleasure with which their parents and grandparents, urged on by questions never asked of them before, describe their life histories.

Sometimes what emerges is shocking and shameful information which can be told only with much hesitation and pain. The students discover that their own life histories can be as those of our clients. They come to realize that while their own lives may be viewed as ruptures with their ancestry, they are, simultaneously, historic continuities, and as such are in a position to bridge banks which seemed very far apart.

Whether or not the student becomes stuck in anger and disappointment towards his own parents seems to be the determinant for his ability to accept and apply Nagy's approach.

Involving themselves fully in the different life histories of the group members sometimes offers the possibility of going further with their own.

Students who eagerly adopt Nagy's concepts as a model to explain their own life courses must guard against reductionism. Otherwise, they are bound to the pitfall of reducing the Contextual approach to the psychological-emotional dimension only.

These explorations of the family explicitly do not have the purpose of therapeutic sessions. They are concrete training exercises in multidirectional partiality. We assume the position of the coach who discourages students from making therapeutic interventions. He takes special care that no one is pressed into disloyalty toward parents or other family members.

It has been obvious, nevertheless, that these procedures can have therapeutic implications. A student's training may enable him or her to make important life decisions. One young woman, for example, had been in a quandary about bearing children. During the presentation of her family of origin, she discovered a new facet of her life story. Spurred by this revelation, she went to her mother to ask if she were capable of being a good mother. After this conversation, the daughter was able to make a distinct choice for herself, and soon afterwards she became pregnant. Years ago it seemed too demanding to require these explorations of the students, but our experiences of the last five years have taught us the contrary.

How often we all feel the desire to pose certain questions to family members, to talk with one's mother or father, brother or sister, about matters which we never understood or which still trouble us in some way. But there is always something which stops us from doing so, always a reason to postpone the matter once again.

For our students that date arrives irrevocably when they present their family tree in the classroom and elucidate their own, unique generational lines with photographs, memorabilia, and stories. They have embarked on journeys into their families' past, sought histories and explanations; often they return with more than they had ever anticipated.

Of course, these discussions require special conditions:

- The group of students cannot be large, preferably not more than eight participants.

- The students should feel secure in the group. Mutual ac-

quaintance and mutual trust should be established
early.

- Each student should expect and receive complete con-
fidentiality from the other members of the group. Note
taking or tape recording during the presentations is
not permitted.

- There should be ample time allotted for this evocation of
the past and for discussion of the material.

- A discussion leader should be present, who can, when
needed, steer and oversee the process. The leader should
be willing to conduct a personal follow-up interview if
the need arises.

The Four-Dimensional Framework

Acquiring knowledge of all systemic forces within a family is in-
dispensable to the beginning family therapist. He or she should
learn which forces to attend to and which to ignore in formulat-
ing a strategy to enter the system.

He must become thoroughly acquainted with all com-
municational, interactional, and transactional patterns of family
phenomena. Without a well-founded knowledge of family systems, a therapist thoroughly trained in individual therapy will
not be able to apply Nagy's working method with families, even
when he is familiar with Nagy's vision. Nor will a family therapist
who knows little about individual therapy be equipped to apply
Nagy's approach.

At the onset of the family therapeutic framework, it seemed
that the new ideas would transcend the restrictions of individual
therapy, but classical family therapy so emphasized the discoveries of family pathology that a new terminology was inven-
ted, and a new set of restrictions came into being. This *four-
dimensional* framework of human relationships forms the foundation of Nagy's effort to do justice, as much as possible, to the total
human image by reducing as little of that image as possible.

Dimension of facts:
Hereditary factors, physical health, adoption, unemployment, disability, etc.

Dimension of needs or psychology:
Basic needs, instincts, defense mechanisms, ego strength, conditioning, dreams, etc.

Dimension of transactions:
Power, competition, coalitions, alliances, etc.

Dimension of relational ethics:
Loyalty, justice, trustworthiness, entitlement, merits, etc.

Two Case Histories

The dimension of relational ethics is the one that is most characteristic of Nagy's approach. We offer no systematic scheme of diagnosis and treatment à la Nagy. Instead we offer a number of guidelines here in the form of two case studies.

Cecile

The family consists of: father, age 35, mechanic; mother, age 33, part-time saleswoman; Cecile, age seven, first grader; Paul, age five, kindergarten.

On the advice of their family doctor, Mr. and Mrs. G sought help at a child guidance clinic for their daughter, Cecile, who had become increasingly unmanageable both at home and in school. Their son Paul presented no behavioral problems. In the initial interview, the social worker was struck immediately by the great concern of both parents. They emphasized strongly how much they welcomed the births of both children and how distressed they were over the problems with their daughter.

Later, in a session with her supervisor, the social worker mentioned incidentally that Mrs. G had severed all ties with her mother during her pregnancy with the oldest child. The supervisor instructed the social worker to pay close attention to this matter because of a possible connection between the rupture with the grandmother and the difficulties which the parents were now experiencing with Cecile. (*Stagnation in the asymmetrical line; presentation of the revolving slate.*) The supervisor also emphasized that the social worker must not be seduced into siding with Mrs. G or allow her to become disloyal to the grandmother by encouraging her to express the negative aspects only in the relation of her life story. (*The principle of multidirected partiality—the ability to side with everyone involved in the relationship, whether or not they are present in the interview.*)

In the next interview, with only Mrs. G present, the following information was revealed: Mrs. G was the younger of two daughters, born 12 years after the birth of her sister. The two daughters were the apples of their father's eye. Their parents had a troubled marriage, and both daughters invariably sided with their father whenever a conflict arose. (*A situation of split loyalty.*)

The grandmother repeatedly threatened suicide. Mrs. G carried the heaviest burden of the tensions because her older sister had left home much earlier to marry. She herself married at age 23. Soon afterwards the grandfather died.

The significant difference in age between the two sisters and the death of the grandfather were both very influential factors in determining the course of the mother's life.

The grandmother fell back wholly on the care of her youngest daughter, Mrs. G, and moved in with her.

As Mrs. G has been raised in a situation of split loyalty, she pays not only the part to which the grandmother is now entitled but, by overpaying, attempts to compensate her for what had been withheld before. By giving her mother her full share, she tries to restore the equilibrium between herself and her parents. This is a very difficult task.

Mrs. G endeavored wholeheartedly to provide for the grandmother, but never felt acknowledged for her efforts. On the contrary, she learned that her mother belittled her in gossip with her sister. (*Lack of acknowledgment engenders continual overpayment.*)

Mr. G did not want to split his wife and mother-in-law and so did not interfere. His noninvolvement prevented a clash between vertical and horizontal loyalties, but provided no support on the horizontal level.

A vehement quarrel between Mrs. G and her sister over a minor issue caused a rupture with the entire family of origin. The grandmother, who was present during the quarrel, declared that she had never loved her youngest daugher, had never wanted her. Mrs. G was shocked and distraught. (*An enormous lack of acknowledgment can lead to destructive entitlement.*)

Following the rupture, the grandmother moved from the home of her youngest daughter to that of her eldest one, who lived in the neighborhood nearby. They encountered each other regularly, on the street or in the supermarket. Mrs. G felt pestered. (*Searching for resources of trust is often masked.*)

Neither of them was able to take openly the first step toward reconciliation. In point of fact, Mrs. G longed for restored contact with the grandmother, a longing that became stronger when she became pregnant. (*Pregnancy reinforces the sense of connectedness in the chain of generations.*)

Soon after giving birth, the mother saw, with shock, the striking resemblance of her newborn child to her own mother. (*Sorrow underlies the manifest anger. Because of the split loyalty, the balance had lost its equilibrium. And the next generation is bound to become involved immediately after birth.*)

Mother did not notify the grandmother after the birth of her daughter and did not visit to show off Cecile. However, she sent flowers to the grandmother for her birthday, and left it for her to respond.

Now a parent herself, Mrs. G can assume the position of an adult—rather than that of a parentified child—in her effort to restore trust.

The grandmother restored the contact. The mother discovered that the grandmother had already begun knitting for her grandchild during the pregnancy. When the grandmother fell seriously ill, she moved once more to the family of her youngest daughter and remained there until her death.

The balance of give-and-take between grandmother and mother had regained its equilibrium. Mrs. G stated that her debt in regard to the rupture had been settled.

The asymmetrical lines of life cross. Her pregnancy gave the mother a natural opportunity to earn entitlement. Nevertheless, she still experienced as a fresh wound the grandmother's claim that she never wanted her. Hurt deeply, she talked about her life's history with such emotion that it seemed the incident had happened yesterday. (*Damage done to the inherent entitlement of the child is hard to repair.*)

The social worker tried to elucidate the grandmother's perspective and to side with her interests; for instance she evoked the grandmother's painful feeling of exclusion from the strong bond between the grandfather and both his daughters. (*Effort to exonerate the grandmother; the principle of multidirected partiality*)

In the next supervisory session, the recommendation was to continue along the same lines. These include: (1) Efforts to find ways *not* to create a static picture of the case history material, shift attention back to the complaints of the child at the time of the referral; (2) maintaining the principles of the fourth dimension (of relational ethics) and not surrendering to the temptation to rely on the second and third dimensions.

In order to halt the destructive process existing throughout the generations, the mother must start her discovery trip to the past. (*Searching for resources of trust and for information which can exonerate the grandmother.*)

The mother apparently knows very little of the grandmother's life history. Where are the sources which can provide the needed information? The grandmother herself is no longer alive, and thus we must locate other people who can tell the mother more about her. When questioned, the mother states that a sister of the grandmother, who had in former days attempted to aid in a mother-daughter reconciliation, is still alive. Thus, it is possible to discuss with this aunt the life of the grandmother and, just as important, the grandmother's feelings at the time of the mother's birth. Are there photographs to be found of the grandmother and mother just after the birth? What can the mother's older sister tell about this period?

Here, again, is the search for resources of trust: Had there been moments at which grandmother had shown real care for her daughter? Events at which both grandparents stood together for the interests of their children? Establishing a posthumous reconciliation would be of eminent importance to the next generation.

Orfee

The second situation deals with the referral of a teenaged girl to an agency for single parents.

Orfee is a girl from Surinam, age 18, who is three months pregnant. She has lost contact with the father. Orfee has had no fixed residency for half a year. She ran away from one of the residential homes in which she had been placed for wayward behavior. Three years ago she left the home of the foster parents with whom she had left Surinam when she was 10 years old.

The mother of Orfee is 36 years of age and lives in Surinam with Orfee's three half-brothers. Contact between mother and daughter is rare. Orfee's father lives in Holland, but she does not know his address. Her upbringing from age one to eight was in the care of the paternal grandmother.

The initial concerns of the referring agency were:

- Helping Orfee to make a decision about her pregnancy. She vacillates between completing and interrupting the pregnancy.

- Helping Orfee to develop the self-confidence necessary for her to make her decision on the basis of her own norms and values and from the viewpoint of her own interests for the future.

Studying the preliminary material from the point of view of

loyalty toward the family of origin leads to the following considerations and action by the agency:

- Running away from foster parents can be an act of invisible loyalty towards one's own parents.

- The wayward behavior may indicate that the foster parents are no better educators than the natural parents. (The foster parents had portrayed the parents as bad people.)

- The mother was also 18 and unmarried when she became pregnant with Orfee. This can be regarded as repetition of known behavior, but which are the underlying, deep, invisible motives springing from principles of loyalty? It could be that Orfee does not want to be better than her mother, does not want to rise above her. By duplicating her actions, she can exonerate her mother.

- In this phase, the father of the child is, for Orfee, of little importance. Her own father played an insignificant role in her childhood.

- Orfee was encouraged to take *action* by contacting her mother by letter or telephone. The mother did not reject these efforts; on the contrary, she told Orfee she had every expectation of Orfee's becoming a good mother for her child.

- This was an important contribution to Orfee's making the decision about her pregnancy. In the ongoing line of the generations the mother in Surinam becomes a prospective grandmother through the unborn child. This engendered in Orfee the realization that she was not isolated or alone, that her pregnancy brought forth new points of rejunction with the past and the future.

Following are considerations and action from the viewpoint of trust and justice:

- Inherent entitlement is at issue, as became obvious from her statement: "If my mother had *forced* me to have an abortion, how could I ever justify my own right to exist?

- The reestablishment of trust between mother and daughter provided Orfee with a new chance to give in what was for her a preeminently vital relationship.

- It would be desirable to reestablish the broken contact with the paternal grandmother, possibly a means of repairing the breach with the grandfather as well. Both grandmother and granddaughter will have the opportunity to make a deposit in the balance of obligation and merit, and their violated sense of justice could be healed.

- In regard to inherent entitlement and the interests of the still unborn child, these are responsible actions by Orfee. If the account between the generations is justly settled, it is no longer likely that the child be caught in the revolving slate in this chain of the generations.

- One further matter requiring attention is the restoration of contact with the foster parents. Moreover, one must consider the relationship of the foster parents with the natural parents.

Orfee, who has chosen to complete her pregnancy, needs to be supported in the following aspects:

- Active, overt loyalty can prevent the undesirable consequences of invisible loyalties. In this instance, it is foreseeable that Orfee could, out of invisible loyalties, send her child to Surinam to be raised by her mother when the child has reached the age of one, the same age at which Orfee herself was sent from her mother to the care of her paternal grandmother.

- Even if attempts to reestablish contact with the father do not provide clearly satisfactory results, the action in itself can be the beginning of a restoration of trust and, as such, have a liberating effect.

- In the first stages of her motherhood, Orfee should be provided with ample assistance in the daily care of her child. As a mother, she should be acknowledged as the most important figure in her baby's life, without making her solely accountable for the consequences and responsibilities. In this case, the foster mother might have an opportunity to lend a helping hand.

Discussion of Cases

We use these two examples to reiterate some crucial points:

Action

1. Action in the form of a personal investment in seeking fairness reaps greater results than resigning oneself to a state of injustice.

2. Actions are fundamental steps for building trust and obtaining health.

3. While a moratorium may sometimes be necessary, it is never a permanent solution. What is often required from the client are courageous, repeated efforts to set in motion once again the balance of justice.

Some Considerations for the Therapist

1. The therapist adheres to the principles of loyalty, justice, and merited trust, evoking the ethical implications even in seemingly helpless situations.

2. The therapist functions in this process as a *coach* and not as a superior parent. He asks: How can we as a team

(therapist and client) cooperate to establish a better relationship with your parents?

3. The therapist's language should be preeminently rejunctive; for instance, he should be able to transform the language of anger to that of responsibility and longing for trust.

4. Without denying pathology, the therapist should direct himself and his clients to discovering and reopening resources of trust.

5. The therapist should always keep his mind on the principle of multidirected partiality, considering the interests of all persons influenced by the therapy, including the following generations.

6. The application of Nagy's methods in the therapist's own practice will be most successful when the therapist has a natural affinity for that approach. If one is to introduce clients to a road leading to a deeper dimension of human existence, one assumes also the *responsibility* of helping them continue along the road and, hopefully, reach the desired destination. Ideally, the therapist will find the inspiration for working along these lines in his own personality; otherwise, his task will prove too burdensome. This is a task not without risks if the principles should be handled artificially. The danger is that the therapist and clients may remain caught in the psychological dimension if the therapist's aims are for insight only, which is in itself insufficient. What counts is one's action toward the other, the effort to engage oneself in a genuine dialogue.

From a Questionnaire Among Students

We sent out a questionnaire to those former students of the advanced training for social workers who had chosen family therapy—including Nagy's methods—as their subject.

The following excerpts reveal that most of the responses we received centered, for the most part, around two inquiries:

1. *What has been the significance of Nagy's approach to you in terms of your own family life and with your family of origin, and how have these personal insights and experiences altered your professional working methods?*

- That I have been able to survey and analyze my own history and that of my family has made me more self-confident. This has had a direct effect on my relationship with my clients.

- The principle of "receiving through giving" has become vitally important to me, both personally and professionally.

- From my personal experiences I have become convinced that a new balance between the generations can develop which frees each participant to give of himself.

- One cannot require from others what one cannot realize oneself. My claim of the ability to help others is founded on my tackling the difficult matters in my own life.

- One of the major reversals in my work since I first became acquainted with Nagy's approach is the shift in my focus from pathology to the search for healthy resources.

- Experiencing for myself the pain involved in handling ruptures within a family has made me modest and sympathetic in my interviews with clients.

- Acknowledgment of each other's interests has brought about new healthy resources in my own family and in my family of origin. I feel as if I myself am a more complete person now.

- I have abandoned the accusatory position from which I had previously regarded my family.

- In former days I complied too readily with the aggression of the children towards the parents; now I try always to see the parents' side as well.

- I pay less attention now to the thoughts and feelings one has about his relationship with the other, and try to concentrate more on discovering the means of stimulating people to become more active in those relationships.

- Overall, I now associate more carefully and consciously with people, both privately and in my work. I am less judgmental; I am more attentive to seeing where the loyalties are. I keep an eye on the balance and consider how I can help, when necessary, in restoring it. As a therapist I have become not only more skillful, but more human.

- Nagy's approach had a great significance for my own family, but I have difficulty in applying it to my clients.

- Although it may seem at first that going back through three generations is a long road to travel, I have found that, ultimately, it is the surest and shortest route to the heart of the matter.

- In cases of divorce in which children are a party, one should keep in mind the relationships which the children have with their grandparents. It is often apparent that the parents have lost sight of this.

2. *Which difficulties do you experience in the application of Nagy's approach?*

- Setting into motion a process of trust-building and genuine mutuality in troubled relationships.

- It is very difficult for me to remain multidirectionally partial (to be able to side sequentially with all parties).

- I am still drawn into siding with the scapegoat in the family.

- How to deal with certain prejudices—such as elderly people being excluded from therapy because they are thought to be too old to change.

- I find Nagy's approach difficult to use in crisis intervention.

- The approach requires much thinking ahead and planning. I am more accustomed to following where the events of the moment lead.

- It is long-term work, and I find myself regularly caught by lack of time.

- It is difficult to make the step from "knowing" to "acting" to allow the client time enough to share with me all the pain of the past, to do so without making him disloyal, and then to sense the right moment for taking action.

- Partners may be too occupied with each other's past. They are often still too angry, and the treatment does not last long enough to establish intergenerational lines.

- I need to develop the creativity necessary to put clients on the scent of their own family history in each new situation.

- I think the most oppressive factor in Nagy's approach is that it seems at times as if returning to the parents' family is the only way to solve even the most elementary problems.

- Nagy's frame of reference functions for me as a kind of general background which is useful in setting up a hypothesis; it is an important tool but it is made too absolute.

- It is hard for me to judge that point in the therapy at which one is ready to broach deeper dimensions.

- Making action rather than insight the issue is the most difficult part of Nagy's method for me.

The discoveries made within the classroom can create the security which encourages the student to undertake this fundamental task with clients. One learns to develop a special sensitivity for the dimension of relational ethics, for discovering signs of possible trust reserves in the relationships even when the indications are at first sight hardly visible.

Obvious stagnations and ruptures have great power of attraction and are perhaps too quickly translated into pathological terms by the traditional therapist. It is preeminently our task as teachers to throw the light of relational ethics on this same material, especially from the point of view which proposes that disappointment, anger, and hatred are always secondary to the desire for trustworthy relationships.

APPENDIX A: SOME DEFINITIONS IN CONTEXTUAL THERAPY BY IVAN BOSZORMENYI-NAGY, M.D.

Context

The entire fabric of prospective resources available for all persons involved in the relationship. It includes the ethics of the individual vantage points of all members, the dialogues between them, the systems of their transactional patterns and transgenerational consequences.

Contextual Therapy

Bases its therapeutic design on the full spectrum (four dimensions) of relational determinants: facts, psychology, transactional systems, and relational ethics.

Dialogue

Beyond its popular usage as conversation or meaningful talk, in Contextual Therapy dialogue means reciprocal accountability and commitment. Dialogue thus extends from a dyadic to a multiperson context: One is in a dialogue with posterity, for example, even if the latter is not able to return one's responsible concern.

Dimensions

These represent fundamental, nonreducible categories of both relational behavior and therapy. The dimensions of facts, psychology, transactions (power), and ethics of reliability are always present in human relationships.

Entitlement

Relational credit, accumulating in the self as a result of due consideration offered to the partner. It is a significant part of fair balancing in asymmetrical (parent-child) relationships. It is different from an arrogant attitude of entitlement and the psychic state of sense of entitlement. Its main effect results in liberation for life and productivity.

Ethics (Relational)

Contextual Therapy is concerned with the ethic of fairness rather than with any ethic of moral values or priorities. What one person does to the partner (support, help, recognition, due concern, exploitation, hurting, etc.) is the subject of this ethics. Specifically, it deals with balances of fairness between relating partners.

Individuation

By individuation is meant a process that forms the person's unique otherness vis-à-vis relating to others. In addition, individuation connotes a process of cohesive personality integration.

Invisible Loyalty

Unintentional incorporation of an indirect repayment to the past through destructiveness toward the self or others; a pathogenic circumstance.

Intergenerational Relationships

An asymmetrical relational context created by reproduction itself. It constitutes the most essential of possible dialogues. Its commitment characteristics are based on the irreversibility of the parent's immediate obligation for caring and the child's evolving obligation for a reciprocal consideration of both the preceding generations and posterity.

Ledger

A calculation of the ethical balance between accumulating merits and debts on two sides of each relationship.

Legacy

Mandates that originate from the earned entitlement of our past, fulfillable in part through concern about the needs of our parents, but mainly through due consideration of the needs of posterity.

Loyalty

A context of relationships invested with merit earned by blood-related kinship or by fair consideration. It is a triadic notion involving the preferential rating of one relational commitment over another.

Loyalty Conflict

A competition between the claims of filial and horizontal (e.g. marital) loyalties.

Moratorium

Moratorium is an important therapeutic principle based on timing of both intervention and expected effects. It is a combination of explicit definition of a therapeutic goal with appropriate patience concerning what each person is ready to do. It combines consistent expectation with the offer of giving appropriate room and time.

Multidirected Partiality

The major methodological attitude of the Contextual therapist aimed at evoking a dialogue of mutual position-taking among family members. It consists of a sequential empathic turning toward, and due crediting of, member after member, directing both acknowledgment and expectation at them, including even the absent members.

Parentification

The consequence of parenting that is deficient because of an exploitative use of the child through his or her own efforts to fulfill the legacy of filial obligation.

Revolving Slate

A substitutive pseudosolution to correct past hurts and victimization via vindictive behavior toward an innocent third party (e.g. one's spouse or child).

Symmetry and Asymmetry

Symmetry deals with the ethics of fairness between people. It pertains to balances of justifiable expectations (e.g., between adult and child), equitability of contributions, and burden of consequences.

APPENDIX B: BIBLIOGRAPHY OF WORKS BY IVAN BOSZORMENYI-NAGY, M.D.

Books

edited with J. L. Framo, *Intensive Family Therapy: Theoretical and Practical Aspects.* New York: Harper & Row, 1965.

with A. S. Freidman, J. E. Jungreis, G. Lincoln, H. E. Mitchell, J. C. Sonne, R. V. Speck & G. Spivak, *Psychotherapy for the Whole Family: Case Histories, Techniques and Concepts of Family Therapy of Schizophrenia in the Home and Clinic.* New York: Springer, 1965.

edited with G. H. Zuk, *Family Therapy and Disturbed Families.* Palo Alto: Science and Behavior Books, 1967.

by the Group for the Advancement of Psychiatry, A *Survey of the Field of Family Therapy.* New York: Committee on the Family, 1969.

with A. Friedman et al., *Therapy with Families of Sexually Acting-Out Girls.* New York: Springer, 1971.

with G. M. Spark, *Invisible Loyalties: Reciprocity in Intergenerational Family Therapy.* New York: Harper & Row, 1973. (Reprinted by Brunner/Mazel, New York, 1984.)

by A. Van Heusden and E. M. Van den Eerenbeemt, *Ivan Boszormeny-Nagy en zijn visie op individuele en gezinstherapie* (Ivan Boszormeny-Nagy and his Vision of Individual and Family Therapy) in Dutch. The Netherlands: DeToorts, Haarlem, 1983.

with B. R. Krasner, *Between Give and Take: A Clinical Guide to Contextual Therapy.* New York: Brunner/Mazel, 1986.

Foundations of Contextual Therapy: The Collected Papers of Ivan Boszormenyi-Nagy. New York: Brunner/Mazel, 1987.

Articles

Formation of phosphopyruvate from phosglycerate in hemolyzed human ethrocytes. *Journal of Biological Chemistry,* 1955, 212(1), 495-499.

with F. J. Gerty, Difference between the phosphorous metabolism of erythrocytes of normals and of patients suffering from schizophrenia. *Journal of Nervous and Mental Disease,* 1955, 121(1), 53-59.

with F. J. Gerty, Diagnostic aspects of a study of intracellular phosphorylations in schizophrenia. *American Journal of Psychiatry,* 1955, 112(1), 11-17.

with J. Kueber, Effect of insulin on the metabolism of phosphorous in human erythrocytes. *Biochemistry and Biophysical Acta,* 1955, 18, 302-303.

with F. J. Gerty & J. Kueber, Correlation between an anomoly of the intracellular metabolism of adenosine nucleotides and schizophrenia. *Journal of Nervous and Mental Disease,* 1956, 124(4), 413-416.

with D. Blackford, Effect of methylene blue on the metabolism of adenine nucleotides in human erythrocytes. *Archives of Biochemistry and Biophysics,* 1956, 65(2), 580-582.

Influence of a magnetic field upon the leucocytes of the mouse. *Nature,* 1956, 177, 577-578.

with F. J. Gerty, Anomaly of the metabolism of adenine nucleotides in the erythrocytes of schizophrenia patients. *Confinia Neurologica,* 1958, 18, 92-96.

Correlations between mental illness and intracellular metabolism. *Confinia Neurologica,* 1958, 18, 88-91.

with M. Hollender, Hallucination as an ego experience. *A.M.A. Archives of Neurology and Psychiatry,* 1958, 80, 93-97.

with J. L. Framo, Hospital organization and family oriented psychotherapy of schizophrenia. *Proceedings of the 3rd World Congress of Psychiatry,* Montreal, June 4-10, 1961, pp. 476-480.

Psychiatric treatment for families. *Lines of Communication* (Newsletter of Mental Health Association of Southeast Pennsylvania), October 1962.

with J. L. Framo & J. Osterweil, A relationship between threat in the manifest content of dreams and active-passive behavior in psychotics. *Journal of Abnormal and Social Psychology,* 1962, 65(1), 41-47.

with J. L. Framo, Family concept of hospital treatment of schizophrenia. In J. H. Masserman (Ed.), *Current Psychiatric Therapy,* Vol 2. New York: Grune & Stratton, 1962, pp. 159-166.

The concept of schizophrenia from the perspective of family treatment. *Family Process,* 1962, 1, 103-113.

with J. L. Framo, Psychotherapy with the family in schizophrenia. *Journal of the Medical Association of Georgia,* 1963, 52(8), 366-367.

with G. H. Zuk & E. Heiman, Some dynamics of laughter in family therapy. *Family Process,* 1963, 2(2), 302-314.

A theory of relationships: Experience and transaction. In I. B.-Nagy & J. L. Framo (Eds.), *Intensive Family Therapy.* New York: Harper & Row, 1965, pp. 33-86. (Reprinted by Brunner/Mazel, New York, 1985.)

Intensive family therapy as process. In I. B-Nagy & J. L. Framo (Eds.), *Intensive Family Therapy.* New York: Harper & Row, 1965, pp. 87-142.

with G. Spivak, The Oracle family. In A. S. Friedman et al. (Eds.), *Psychotherapy for the Whole Family: Case Histories, Techniques and Concepts of Family Therapy of Schizophrenia in the Home and Clinic.* New York: Springer, 1965, pp. 106-129.

The concept of change in conjoint family therapy. In A. S. Friedman et al.

(Eds.), *Psychotherapy for the Whole Family: Case Histories, Techniques and Concepts of Family Therapy of Schizophrenia in the Home and Clinic.* New York: Springer, 1965, pp. 305-319.

Families of schizophrenics found responsive to therapy in home setting. *Psychiatric Progress,* November 1965, p. 6.

with B. S. Vanderheiden, Preparation of 32p-labeled nucleotides. *Analytical Biochemistry,* 1965, 13, 496-504.

From family therapy to a psychology of relationships: Fictions of the individual and fictions of the family. *Comprehensive Psychiatry,* 1966, 7(5), 408-423.

Relational modes and meaning. In G. Zuk & I. B-Nagy (Eds.), *Family Therapy and Disturbed Families.* Palo Alto: Science Behavior Books, 1967, pp. 58-73.

Types of pseudo individuation. In N. Ackerman et al. (Eds.), *Expanding Theory and Practice in Family Therapy.* New York: Family Service Association of America, 1967, pp. 66-69.

Communication versus internal programming of relational attitudes. In N. Ackerman et al. (Eds.), *Expanding Theory and Practice in Family Therapy.* New York: Family Service Association of America, 1967, pp. 89-92.

Assumptions of a theory of relationships. *Psychotherapy and Psycho-Somatics,* 1968, 16, 296-297.

with other members of the Committee on the Family, Conceptual framework. In *The Field of Family Therapy.* New York: Group for the Advancement of Psychiatry, 1970, 7(78), 562-571.

Review of Helm Stierlin's "Conflict and Reconciliation," *Family Process,* 1970, 9(1), 105-108.

Critical incidents in the context of family therapy. In N. Ackerman (Ed.), *Family Therapy, International Psychiatry Clinics.* Boston: Little, Brown, 1970, 7, 4, 251-260.

The use of external social control in family therapy. In A. S. Friedman et al. (Eds.), *Therapy with Families of Sexually Acting-Out Girls.* New York: Springer, 1971, pp. 187-197.

Foreword. In J. L. Framo (Ed.), *Family Interaction: A Dialogue Between Family Researchers and Family Therapists.* New York: Springer, 1972.

with C. Kramer, M. Bowen, A. Ferber, A. Leader, C. Whitaker, Being and becoming a family therapist. In A. Ferber, M. Mendelsohn, A. Napier (Eds.), *The Book of Family Therapy.* New York: Science House, 1972, pp. 134-154.

with C. Kramer, M. Bowen, A. Ferber, A. Leader, C. Whitaker, How I became a family therapist. In A. Ferber, M. Mendelsohn, A. Napier (Eds.), *The Book of Family Therapy.* New York: Science House, 1972, pp. 84-85.

Loyalty implications of the transference model in psychotherapy. *A.M.A. Archives of General Psychiatry,* 1972, 27, 374-380.

Ethical and practical implications of intergenerational family therapy. *Journal of Psychotherapy and Psychosomatics,* 1974, 24, 261-268. Also in J. G. Howells (Ed.), *Advances in Family Psychiatry,* Vol, I. New York: International Universities Press, 1979.

Forebyggelse og Dynamikk i Familierelasjoner. *Fokus pa Familien,* 1974, 2(3), 3-8.

Family therapy: Its meaning for mental health. *Science News Quarterly,* 1975, 1(4), 1-3.

Dialectic view of intergenerational family therapy. Presented at the 4th International Symposium on Family Therapy in Zurich, Switzerland, Sept. 30-Oct. 4, 1975.

Comments on Helm Stierlin's "Hitler as the Bound Delegate of His Mother. *"History of Childhood Quarterly: The Journal of Psychohistory,* 1976, 3(4), 500-505.

Behavior change through family change. In A. Burton (Ed.), *What Makes Behavior Change Possible?* New York: Brunner/Mazel, 1976, 227-258.

with N. Gansheroff & J. Matrullo, Clinical and legal issues in the family therapy record. *Hospital and Community Psychiatry,* 1977, 28, 911-913.

Depth and paradox in marital relationships. In G. Pirooz Sholevar (Ed.), *Changing Sexual Values and the Family,* Springfield, IL: Charles C Thomas, 1977, pp. 70-73.

Mann und Frau: Verdienstkonten in den Geschlechtsrollen. *Familiendynamik,* Jahrgang 2, 1977, 1-10.

Guidelines for the contextual evaluation and management of child abuse cases. In *How to Handle a Child Abuse Case: A Manual for Attorneys Representing Children.* Published by Support Center for Child Advocates, Inc. and the Committee on Child Abuse, Young Lawyers Section of the Philadelphia Bar Association, 1978.

with B. Krasner (Ed.), Gruppenloyalitat als Motiv fur Politischen Terrorismus. *Familiendynamik,* Juli 1978, 199-208.

Review of H. Stierlin, *Psychoanalysis and Family Therapy: Selected Papers. American Journal of Psychiatry,* 1978, 135, 1011.

Vision dialectica de la terapia familiar intergeneractional. *Terapia Familiar,* 1978, 2, 90-110.

Interview with the editor on the status of the field of family therapy. *Terapia Familiar,* 1979, 187-198.

Contextual therapy: Therapeutic leverages in mobilizing trust. Report 2, Unit IV. *The American Family.* Philadelphia: The Continuing Education Service of Smith, Kline and French Laboratories, 1979.

with D. Bloch, M. Bowen, S. Minuchin, I. Zwerling, Family Therapy: Resources for change. Report 5, Unit IV. *The American Family.* Philadelphia: The Continuing Education Service of Smith, Kline and French Laboratories, 1979.

Ethics of human relationships and the treatment contract. In H. L. Lennard & S. C. Lennard (Eds.), *Ethics of Health Care.* New York: Gondolier, 1979, pp. 53-66.

Entitlement and accountability: The ethical balance in relationships. In H. L. Lennard & S. C. Lennard (Eds.), *Ethics of Health Care.* New York: Gondolier, 1979, pp. 90-100.

Principles of the ethics of intervention. In H. L. Lennard & S. C. Lennard (Eds.), *Ethics of Health Care.* New York: Gondolier, 1979, pp. 120-136.

with B. Krasner, Trust-based therapy: A contextual approach. *American Journal of Psychiatry,* 1980, 137, 767-775.

with D. Ulrich, Contextual family therapy. In A. Gurman & P. Kniskern (Eds.), *Handbook of Family Therapy.* New York: Brunner/Mazel, 1981, pp. 159-186.

with other members Committee on the Family, Recommendations to the courts. In *Divorce, Child Custody and the Family*. Group for the Advancement of Psychiatry Report. New York: Mental Health Materials Center, 1980.

Clinical and legal issues in the family therapy record. In D. Rosenthal (Ed.), *Family Therapy Readings*. Springfield, IL: Charles C Thomas, 1981.

with B. R. Krasner, The contextual approach to psychotherapy. In G. Berenson & H. White (Eds.), *Annual Review of Family Therapy*. New York: Human Sciences Press, 1981, 1, 92-128.

by G. Reich, G. Baethga & K. Deisler, Ivan B. Nagy interviewed in Gottingen, November 25, 1981. *Context*, a journal of the German Family Therapy Association, in press.

with M. Cotroneo & B. R. Krasner, The contextual approach to child custody decisions. In P. G. Sholevar (Ed.), *The Handbook of Marriage and Marital Therapy*. New York: Spectrum Publications, 1981, pp. 475-480.

Contextual therapy: The realm of the individual, an interview by Margaret Markham. *Psychiatric News*, 1981, XVI, 20 & 21.

Contextual therapy: Therapeutic leverages in mobilizing trust. In R. J. Green & J. L. Framo (Eds.), *Family Therapy: Major Contributions*. New York: International Universities Press, 1981, pp. 393-415.

L. Wynne, first author, with A. Gurman, R. Ravich & I. B. Nagy, The family and marital therapies. In J. M. Lewis & G. Usdin (Eds.), *Treatment Planning in Psychiatry*. Washington, DC: American Psychiatric Association, 1982, pp. 225-285.

Suicide attempts: Is family therapy most effective? Review of a speech presented at the American Suicidology Society meeting, April 17, 1982. *Frontiers of Psychiatry Roche Report*, 1982, 12, 8, 4-5.

Commentary: Transgenerational Solidarity: Therapy's Mandate and Ethics. *Family Process*, 1985, 24, 454-456.

Transgenerational Solidarity: The Expanding Context of Therapy and Prevention. *American Journal of Family Therapy*, 1985, 14, 195-212.

Contextual Therapy and the Unity of Therapies. In S. Sugarman (Ed.), *The Interface of Individual and Family Therapy*, Rockville, MD: Aspen Publishers, 1986, pp. 65-76.

The Context of Consequences and the Limits of Therapeutic Responsibility. In H. Stierlin, F. B. Simon, & G. Schmidt (Eds.), *Familiar Realities: The Heidelberg Conference*, New York: Brunner/Mazel, 1987, pp. 41-51.

INDEX

Note: Page numbers in *italics* are terms defined in Appendix A.

DATE DUE